Heroes of Mexico

Heroes of Mexico

by

Morris Rosenblum

Fleet Press Corporation
New York

ACKNOWLEDGMENTS

Thanks are due to Mrs. Bea Rosenblum, student of motion-picture history, and Miss Harriet Wingreen, concert pianist, for valuable information about Mexican and Mexican-American celebrities.

For their help in obtaining illustrative material I am indebted to Mr. Lyle Collins, Instituto Allende, San Miguel de Allende, Mexico; Señorita Elsa García González, Secretary to Carlos Chávez; Mrs. Virginia P. Hoke, El Paso Public Library; Mr. Michael C. Luckman, The New School for Social Research; Señor Enrique Best Monterde, Regional Museum, Querétaro, Mexico; Mrs. Esther Panzer, art connoisseur; Mr. Norman Robbins, National Screen Service; Miss May Sinclair, Mexican National Tourist Council, New York City; and Mr. Jason Wingreen.

I am especially grateful to Mr. Maxwell Nurnberg for his valuable suggestions.

Finally I wish to express my deep appreciation to my wife, Dora J. Rosenblum, who covered many a kilometer with me in Mexico, patiently read this work while it was in progress, helped choose the illustrations, and contributed from her store of knowledge of Spanish.

Morris Rosenblum

October, 1969
New York City

EXPLANATION OF SPANISH TITLES AND FAMILY NAMES

Titles

Don—to show respect for a man, usually a person of quality or a gentleman, *Don* (or *don*) is used before his first name.

Doña—used before her first name to show respect for a married or single woman.

Señor—Mister or sir. Señor José Valles = Mr. José Valles. Sí, señor = Yes, sir.

Señores—gentlemen. Used when referring to more than one señor.

Señora—Mrs. or Madame, used before a married woman's name.

Señoras—refers to more than one señora. *Señoras* also = Ladies, as when addressing a group. In religious names, *Señora* = Lady. *Nuestra Señora de Dolores* = Our Lady of Sorrows.

Señorita—Miss or Mademoiselle, used before the name of a young or unmarried woman; also means young lady. Señorita Margarita = Miss Margaret. Sí, señorita = Yes, Miss.

Family Names

A man's full name consists of his first name, or baptismal name, his father's family name, plus the Spanish word *y* ("and") and his mother's family name—in that order. For example, Señor Juárez marries Señorita García; they have a son whom they call Benito. His full name becomes Benito Juárez y García. The son may drop *y García* and be known as Benito Juárez. (Some men drop only *y* and keep both the father's and the mother's family names, as in the name of President Gustavo Díaz Ordaz.)

A woman gets her full name the same way as a man. When she marries, she drops *y* plus her mother's family name, and instead takes her husband's family name plus *de* ("of") in front of it. One of Benito's sisters was named Rosa; her full name was Rosa Juárez y García. When she married José Jiménez, her new name became Rosa Juárez de Jiménez.

The word *de* in a man's name may tell where his family once came from or a well-known family to which it was once related, as Don Quijote de la Mancha, or Ponce de León, or Antonio de Mendoza.

Contents

1

WHO ARE THE HEROES OF MEXICO?

There are about five million Mexican-Americans in the United States of America. They form the second largest minority group in this country. More than two million of them live in California, and about a million and a half in Texas.

A great many Mexican-Americans are very poor. They work for little pay and live in miserable houses. They are Americans but feel they are treated as if they were not part of this country and that little attention is paid to their problems.

Most of the people in Mexico itself have faced similar problems for many years. By knowing more about the Mexicans and Mexico, Americans will better understand the people and their problems and will also get to know the Mexican-Americans better. This book was written so that you may learn more about the land and people of Mexico through the lives of men and women who are called "Heroes of Mexico."

Famous Mexicans and Mexican-Americans in the United States

A number of persons of Mexican origin have become well-known to Americans, especially through their work in this country in art, music, the dance, the theater and movies, on the radio and TV, and also in sports.

Some returned to Mexico, others remained here. Dolores Del Rio, once called the most beautiful woman in the movies, now lives near Mexico City. Once in a while she still acts in an American film. Lupe Velez, Ramon Novarro, and Gilbert Roland are famous names in motion picture history. Tito Guizar sang in opera, gave many recitals, and appeared in Mexican and American pictures. The popular movie star Katy Jurado was born in Mexico. The noted actor Anthony Quinn was born there also, of an Irish father and a Mexican mother. Other familiar names of stars born in Mexico are Margo (full name María Margarita Guadalupe Bolado y Castilla), Pedro Armendáriz, and Ricardo and Carlos Montalbán, brothers. José Limón is one of the great names in modern dancing and ballet.

Dolores Del Rio

Lee Trevino, a Texan of Mexican ancestry, won the U.S. Open golf championship in 1968. Trini (short for Trinidad) Lopez is another famous Texan of Mexican ancestry. This very popular entertainer was born of poor Mexican parents in Dallas, Texas. His records have been among the Top Ten since 1963.

Cantinflas

Here we pay honor to Rafael Osuna, "king of Mexican tennis," winner of the United States singles title at Forest Hills in 1963, and leader or member of teams in many tournaments. At the age of 30, he met a tragic death in an airplane crash on June 4, 1969.

The Hero of the "Little People"

The great comedian Cantinflas (real name Mario Moreno) has long been the most popular movie actor in Latin America. He became known to millions all over the world for his part in *Around the World in Eighty Days*. In Mexican films he used to play the part of an underdog of the slums but later played a great many different roles, such as a rich man, a scientist, a politician, one of the Three Musketeers, a bullfighter, a policeman, and a detective. He is so talented that he could play either a comic Sherlock Holmes or Dr. Watson, either Don Quixote or Sancho Panza.

Cantinflas has been called the Mexican Charlie Chaplin but Chaplin himself has said that Cantinflas is the greatest comedian in the world! Unlike Charlie Chaplin, Cantinflas comes out on top—the winner. This made him loved by the poor of Mexico because there are so many of them. Diego Rivera designed a mural of this beloved man on the front of the Theater of the Insurgents in Mexico City. It shows Cantinflas getting money from the rich and giving it to the poor. The crowds that come to see Cantinflas think about him in that way—that he is one of them. They feel that he is really Mexico, that his making fun of authority and standing up to it, are part of the same fight put up by the Mexicans from Cuauhtémoc against Cortés down through the War of Independence and the Revolution of 1910. He is the kind of hero that the "little people" dream of being, but everybody loves him for his "gift of laughter."

What Is a Hero?

In a certain way, these persons are heroes and heroines. They have accomplished great things and have brought fame not only to themselves but also to their country.

A hero or a heroine is not only a man or a woman who wins glory by fighting bravely on the battlefield. A hero may be a person who struggles for a noble idea against great odds. A hero may be a person who has made the world a better place by his knowledge, teachings, writings, or by any other work, such as art, music, medicine, and physical science.

Worker tilling soil

12

Unnamed and Unknown Heroes

There are heroes in every country whose names do not appear in any books. They can be seen in Mexico trudging for miles, barefoot, on steep mountain roads and on unpaved village streets, carrying heavy loads to the markets or back to their homes. Others work hard all day in the fields. Most of them are Indians, living and toiling almost in the same way as their ancestors did centuries ago. Other unknown heroes can be found working in the factories and shops, or can be seen in the country schools patiently bringing learning to the poor.

The Mexican people have struggled, and have rebelled to gain a better life. Some of the known heroes have tried to bring this to the unknown heroes, often at the risk, and even at the cost, of their own lives.

2

THE LAND FROM WHICH THESE HEROES CAME

Mexico and Its People

Mexico is our nearest southern neighbor. Part of it is situated below the Rio Grande. Mexico borders on Texas, New Mexico, Arizona, and California, all of which once belonged to it. The Mexicans use the word *California* in Baja California, which we call Lower California. *Baja* means low in Spanish, the official language of Mexico.

The official name of Mexico has *United States* in it, since it is *Estados Unidos Mexicanos*, "Mexican United States." All the people of North and South America are Americans. To the Mexicans we are *Norteamericanos*, or North Americans, and our country is the United States of America. However, following the usual style in this country, we use the terms *Americans* and *United States* in this book when we refer to ourselves and our country.

In 1967, the population of Mexico was about forty-six million, with about 70% mestizos (half-breeds), of mixed Spanish and Indian blood. A small number are Spanish-Negro and Negro-Indian mestizos. The Spanish conquerors and later colonizers of Mexico brought along Negro slaves. About 28% of the people are Indians. The remaining 2% are foreigners.

Nine out of ten people speak Spanish, but almost fifty different

National Seal of Mexico

Indian languages are spoken, chiefly Nahuatl (also called Mexican), the tongue of the Aztecs and a few other ancient tribes. At least three million Indians do not speak any Spanish. About 98% of the people are Roman Catholics.

The Geography of Mexico

Mexico is the largest country between the United States and South America. It is a beautiful country with magnificent mountains including high volcanic peaks, of which the best known are Orizaba, Popocatépetl ("Smoking Mountain"), and Ixtaccíhuatl ("White Woman," also known as the "Sleeping Lady"). The chief mountain ranges are the Eastern Sierra and the Western Sierra. There are many famous beaches and resorts, like Acapulco.

Because of the different altitudes the climate varies from tropical to cold. Along the coast and in the lowlands it is very hot, while in Mexico City, about 7,500 feet high, the average temperature is between 65 and 75 degrees all year round. There is a season of light rains between May and October.

The different climate and altitude allow many different things to grow. Food staples are barley, beans, corn, or maize, and wheat. Tropical fruits like bananas add to the diet, as do coffee, rice, and sugar. The cacao tree yields cocoa and chocolate, and jams are made from guava. Among the important products for industry and trade are oil, silver, gold, copper, lead, gems, lumber, cotton, rubber, chicle used for making gum, and sisal, a fiber used for making heavy cord and twine.

Early History of Mexico

Mexico was settled by Indian tribes many centuries ago. The oldest civilization in the Western Hemisphere was that of the Olmecs, who lived in southern Mexico about 3,000 years ago!

Further north were the Toltecs, who were great builders. Much of their work can still be seen in Tula, their capital, and in Teotihuacán. In the south, the Mayas lived in Honduras, Guatemala, and Yucatán. The ruins of their splendid buildings can be seen in Chichén Itzá and Uxmal. In the state of Oaxaca are glorious ruins of structures put up by the Zapotec Indians in Mitla and Monte Albán, their holy cities.

The Aztecs were the most powerful people in Mexico from about 1300 to 1521. They were also called the Mexicas from one of their branches. The name of the country, *Mexico*, which is said to mean Middle of the Moon, is supposed to come from *Mexica* or from *Mexitli*, one of the names of the chief god of the Aztecs. The Aztecs came down from the north, conquered the Toltecs, and extended their empire from the far north to Guatemala.

Mexico under the Spaniards

In 1521, the Spaniards, led by Hernando Cortés, came to Mexico, conquered the Aztecs, and eventually ruled over all of Mexico, Central America, and parts of southwestern United States, which they called New Spain. From 1535 to 1821, New Spain was governed by viceroys, representing the King or Queen of Spain.

Don Antonio de Mendoza

The birthplace of printing
in Mexico

Don Antonio de Mendoza, the first viceroy (1535-1550), protected the Indians' right to hold *ejidos*, or pieces of land owned in common. He built the first schools and colleges in the New World. Indians were allowed to go to these schools, and many became brilliant students and teachers. Mendoza also introduced the printing press in Mexico.

The next viceroy, Don Luis de Velasco (1550-1564), was called "The Emancipator" and "Father of the Indians," because he protected their rights. He founded the University of Mexico. There were in all sixty-one viceroys. Most of them did nothing for the Indians or did them harm. They let the Spaniards make slaves of the Indians and take away their land.

General Iturbide, "The Liberator," but an "Almost-Hero"

In 1821, after the struggles by Hidalgo, Morelos, and other patriots, Spanish rule came to an end in Mexico. General Agustín de Iturbide, who fought at first on the side of the Viceroy, changed sides, and helped overthrow the Spanish. He had himself declared Emperor, but ruled for less than a year. Forced to give up the throne and sent away from the country, he returned a little more than a year later, and was shot as a traitor on July 19, 1824.

Iturbide's life and end are typical of what happened to a number of leaders in Mexican history. They changed sides, often to further their own interests. Iturbide might be called an "almost-hero." However, he is a hero to some Mexicans, and on his tomb in the cathedral in Mexico City there are the Spanish words for "Hero," "Author of Mexican Independence," and "The Liberator."

An "almost-hero" is a person who has performed a great or heroic deed, something good for his country that has endeared him to the people, but who later acted differently. He either changed his ways and brought harm to his country, or he was unable to live up to his early promise of a great career.

Presidents and Heroes, Dictators and "Almost-Heroes"

General Guadalupe Victoria, a hero of the War of Independence, became the first elected president of Mexico in 1824. His rule was followed by unrest, disorder, and civil war for many years. Some presidents were unable to finish their terms. Others came into office by force. Military dictators often held power, and many leaders were assassinated.

17

General Antonio López de Santa Anna

In 1832, General Antonio López de Santa Anna (or Ana) was elected president, but after a year he became dictator. His was a career of ins and outs and eventual failure. He finally died in poverty in 1876, a forgotten man. Yet, like Iturbide, with whom he had fought for independence, he was an "almost-hero." In fact, he was called the "Hero of Tampico" and the "Hero of Veracruz."

Santa Anna was at the head of the troops that stormed the Alamo in the Texan War. He had the garrison, including Davy Crockett, killed. In this war he was defeated by Sam Houston. As a result, Mexico lost Texas. Later, through war with the United States, and by a treaty in which the United States paid for more territory, Mexico lost all of New Spain north of the Rio Grande. Santa Anna had taken part in a revolt against a dictator, but in the end his desire for power and his loss of Mexican territory made him known as "the most hateful man in Mexican history."

Benito Juárez, considered by many the greatest of all Mexicans, was President from 1858 to 1872, with interruptions caused by civil war and foreign invasions. (See Chapter 13.)

After the death of Juárez in 1872, a few more presidents were elected, including General Porfirio Díaz (1877-1880). General Díaz may also be called an "almost-hero." In his younger days he had fought on the side of Juárez against the French and Maximilian, who had invaded Mexico and taken power from 1862 to 1867. In 1884, Díaz was elected President again. By force he remained in office until 1911. He allowed foreign companies into Mexico, where they took over a number of industries, including oil. Finally he was driven from office by a revolt, when he was 80 years old.

Then came the election of Francisco Madero, another "almost-hero." He was a rich man who had good ideas and dared to oppose Díaz whom he helped drive out. At first Madero was very popular, but he proved to be incapable. He was assassinated; some think by order of a trusted man who had helped him, General Victoriano Huerta, and who then became dictator. In 1914, Huerta was driven out of office. A struggle followed with Venustiano Carranza, Alvaro Obregón, Pancho Villa, and Emiliano Zapata as the leaders. The fight that began near the end of Díaz's rule is known as the Revolution of 1910.

Finally, peace came in 1920 with the election of General Obregón. A new constitution had been established under President Carranza in 1917 to bring benefits to the people. Later presidents, like Lázaro Cárdenas (1934-1940) and Adolfo Ruiz Cortines (1952-1958) set good examples that have been followed to this day.

The president of Mexico is elected every six years by direct popular vote. Women have the right to vote. The president may serve only once. He is assisted by a Council and a Congress of two Houses, the Deputies and the Senate. Mexico has 29 states, two territories, and a federal district, in which Mexico City, the capital, is situated.

Problems and Progress

Like other countries of North and South America, including our own, Mexico has its problems. A large part of the population is poor. Many of them work in the fields and would like to own their own piece of land. On the other hand, with the growth of tourism and new industries, the number of millionaires has doubled since World War II (1939-1945). The differences between rich and poor, poverty and great wealth, led in the past to hatred, civil wars, and revolutions. But now, progress is being made in land reform and social security.

The greatest campaign in progress is to educate the one-third of the people who cannot read or write. Children must attend school until they are fifteen. The new slogans in Mexico are "Knowledge is power" and "To educate is to set free."

3

QUETZALCOATL

A GOD AND A HUMAN BEING

The quetzal, or quezal, whose name comes from Nahuatl, an ancient Mexican-Indian language, is a beautiful bird found in Central America and Mexico. The upper part of its plumage is a rich and splendid bronze-green, and the lower part is a brilliant green. The tail feathers of the male have streamers more than two feet long. *Coatl*, from the same language as *quetzal*, means a serpent.

Joined together, these two Indian words form *Quetzalcoatl*, meaning Plumed Serpent, the name of one of the principal gods of some of the ancient Mexican Indians. He was the god of the wind and air, the master of life, a creator and civilizer who loved and benefited mankind. He hated war and human sacrifices. For bringing moisture to the earth, making it rich, and helping crops to grow, he was beloved by farmers.

Quetzalcoatl was the god of astronomy, the science of the stars and planets, and also of astrology, or foretelling the future by the stars and planets. He was the inventor of the calendar. In fact, the ancient Mexican Indians, notably the Aztecs and Mayas, had thought up perfect calendars. One of the great monuments of the past is the stone called *Piedra del Sol*, "Stone of the Sun,"

"Stone of the Sun," the Aztec Calendar

showing the Aztec calendar. Renowned as the god of wisdom and learning, Quetzalcoatl taught men various skills, such as writing, and working in metals like silver and gold.

Quetzalcoatl had an enemy, a fierce god named Texcatlipoca, or Smoking Mirror, who drove Quetzalcoatl away from the central plateau. Before he left, he declared that he would return some day.

The Indian artists painted Quetzalcoatl in many forms. He is often shown as a white man or a white god, sometimes as an old man with white hair and a long beard. He is tall, has a large body, and wears a long robe. Sometimes he is shown simply as a serpent; at other times, he appears as a warrior-god with a bird's beak. He is also pictured with the bright feathers of the quetzal on his head and with different forms of the serpent, especially with fangs and teeth showing through an opening in a mask. In the ruins of

Quetzalcoatl Temple, Tenochtitlán

22

temples many stone carvings of quetzal plumes rising above a serpent's head are found.

Quetzalcoatl was worshiped by many tribes, especially the Toltecs, whose empire was overthrown by the Aztecs in about 1300. The Aztecs had their own gods, but like many ancient conquerors, they took over the vanquished people's gods. That is how Quetzalcoatl became one of the Aztec gods.

There are different legends about Quetzalcoatl, but all agree that he had once been a human being, and that he had led so remarkable and upright a life that he was placed among the gods after his death. Both as a god and as a human being his qualities and accomplishments were very much alike.

He was supposed to have lived at some time between 950 and 1150, the son of Mixcoatl, chief of the Toltecs. Mixcoatl was murdered by his own brother, who then seized the leadership of the tribe. Mixcoatl's wife, who was bearing a child, escaped, and fled to another city, where she died while giving birth to a son. Before she died, she declared that the boy was of divine origin. He was different from other Toltecs in another way since he had a light complexion.

The boy was named Ce Acatl Toplitzin (or Topiltzin), meaning Our Prince Who Was Born on Ce Acatl. Ce Acatl, marked by one reed in the Toltec and Aztec calendar, was the name of a particular year that came every fifty-two years.

His grandparents took care of the boy, who was sent to a religious school when he grew older. There he showed such extraordinary ability in his studies, such amazing wisdom, and such enormous religious devotion that the priests honored him with the title *Quetzalcoatl*, usually given to very wise and learned priests.

Later, Quetzalcoatl, as he was now called, returned to his homeland, dug up his father's body, and buried it in Tula, the Toltec capital, with the respect and honor belonging to a chief. Then he avenged his father's murder by sacrificing his uncle, the murderer, in a sacred fire. The Toltecs made Quetzalcoatl their king and high priest.

At that time, the Toltecs were not a highly civilized people. They were warlike, and worshiped Texcatlipoca, an evil force, who, they believed, had the power to destroy the earth. They feared him so greatly that they offered him human sacrifices to keep him from harming them.

Columns of temple ruins at Tula

Quetzalcoatl began to change their ways. First he brought in artisans, skilled workers, from another tribe. They carved great statues and built huge temples. He also kept his people from making war and encouraged them to cultivate the fields, to work with metals and jade, to weave, and to make pottery. The arts of weaving, making baskets, and doing fine work with semi-precious stones have continued in Mexico to this day.

As a young man, Quetzalcoatl had followed the religion of the Toltecs by making a human sacrifice. As their king and high priest, he changed and became mild. He tried to do away with human sacrifices and became a lover of nature and all living things. Human sacrifices were part of the religion of many ancient peoples, especially the Mexican Indians. They believed that the gods had created man and the earth with their own blood, and that men had to keep the gods strong by giving blood back. Often, Indian tribes, like the Aztecs, made wars just to take captives whom they could sacrifice to the gods.

Quetzalcoatl did not believe in this cruel practice. His stopping of the sacrifices made enemies of many of the priests and other Toltecs who wanted to keep the old ways. Either they called upon Texcatlipoca to help them, and he managed by a trick to make Quetzalcoatl run away from his country, or else the priests stirred up a civil war in which Quetzalcoatl was defeated.

Quetzalcoatl and some of his followers made their way south to Cholula, about 125 miles from Tula. There he taught the inhabitants, the Mixtecs, to write in a picture language and to build temples. At one time Cholula had about 400 temples, most of which were replaced with churches in later times. There is a saying that Cholula has a church for every day in the year. One exists today on the great pyramid built in honor of Quetzalcoatl.

After he had been in Cholula for twenty years, either Texcatlipoca or Quetzalcoatl's personal enemies forced the Mixtecs to drive him away. From Cholula, he went with his followers to Coatzacoalcos on the Gulf of Mexico. Most of his followers went on to Yucatán, the land of the Mayas, who worshiped a god named Kukulcan. His name also means Quetzal Snake, or Plumed Serpent, and many of his qualities were like those of Quetzalcoatl. Many scholars believe that the Mayan civilization is related to the Toltec.

After spending some time in Coatzacoalcos, Quetzalcoatl built a small boat bearing a design of serpents and quetzal feathers. He said farewell to his followers and sailed off to the east. Just like the god Quetzalcoatl, he declared that he would return, and named the date, Ce Acatl. He also promised to restore his ancient kingdom, and his promise was remembered by the Indians of Mexico. Montezuma II, emperor of the Aztecs, thought it was being carried out when the Spaniards came to Mexico from the east.

Mayan Ruins, Yucatán

4

MONTEZUMA

THE AZTEC EMPEROR
CONQUERED BY THE SPANIARDS

In 1502, Montezuma II, a young man of 22, became emperor of the Aztecs. He was the son of a former ruler, but he did not immediately succeed his father. Among the Aztecs the son of an emperor did not necessarily inherit the throne upon his father's death. A council of four nobles chose the new emperor; usually they did pick somebody from the royal family.

The name *Moctezuma* is more generally found today, but we prefer to use the older and more familiar form, *Montezuma*, that we learned long ago.

Before he became emperor, Montezuma studied the lives and ways of the gods. He believed greatly in omens, strange sights and events, like the appearance of a comet or an unusual animal. Although he was known as "a philosopher-king," at the beginning of his reign he was also a warrior.

Montezuma ruled over a rich and mighty empire. His store-houses contained vast treasures of gold and silver, jewelry, priceless gems, and cloths embroidered with gold. Taxes in the form of food, gold and silver, and other valuables came to him from conquered tribes all over Mexico.

The chief city of the Aztecs, really a city-state, was Tenochtitlán. The wandering Aztec-Mexica tribe had been told by their priests to settle where they saw an eagle sitting on a cactus and eating a snake. They came across this sight on a swamp surrounded by water. Here they built their city in about 1325, where Mexico City now stands. The national seal of Mexico shows an eagle, a cactus, and a serpent.

The Aztecs filled in part of the land. They left waterways and a lake around one part of the city. They built bridges over the water and causeways. From the heights of nearby Chapultepec an aqueduct brought fresh drinking water.

The lake was filled with canoes; many of the houses were built along the waterfront or even over the water. There were marketplaces filled with goods and crowded with people. When the Spaniards first saw the great buildings and other sights of Tenochtitlán, they were overcome with wonder and admiration. Soldiers who had seen the truly great cities of Europe said that they had never seen one so rich and splendid as Tenochtitlán. The city looked like a marvelous dream to them; they wondered whether it could be real!

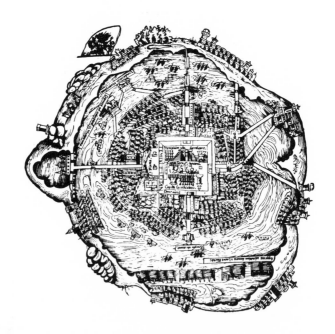

Plan of Tenochtitlán

28

In spite of his wealth and power Montezuma was not really happy. Sometimes he was cheerful, but most of the time he was sad. Strange things happened while he was ruler, and because he believed so much in omens, the supernatural, and fate, he felt that something dreadful was going to happen to him and his kingdom, and that nothing could be done about it.

In eight years, from 1509 to 1517, at least eight strange happenings disturbed Montezuma's peace of mind. A fiery comet was seen, one temple burst into flames, and another was struck by lightning. Fire flashed in the sky by day, and the water of the lake boiled over. Every night an invisible woman could be heard crying, saying over and over, "We are lost. Where can we hide, my children? We must run from the city." A strange bird wearing a mirror on its head was captured in a net by fishermen. When Montezuma looked into the mirror, he saw stars at noon. He looked again, and saw strange men making war while riding on animals that looked like deer. He showed the mirror to his magicians and other men, but nobody saw anything strange in it. Two-headed men were picked up in the street, but when they were taken before Montezuma, they mysteriously vanished.

Montezuma asked his priests, soothsayers, or persons who foretell the future, and sorcerers, persons who work magic, to tell him what these strange things meant. Nobody could give him an answer. No one else had seen any of the omens!

Then the Spaniards began to come to Mexico. In 1511, they conquered Cuba, only a few hundred miles from Yucatán and the small islands near it, like Cozumel. Governor Diego Velázquez of Cuba sent an expedition toward that part of Mexico in 1517 and again in 1518, first to explore and trade, and then to seek gold. Both expeditions failed.

Montezuma had learned about these two voyages. He began to think about the promises made by the "white god" Quetzalcoatl that he would return to Mexico from the east. Montezuma was sure that Quetzalcoatl was on his way back, or was sending his followers, either men or gods. His belief was made stronger by the fact that the year Ce Acatl, the one in which Quetzalcoatl had said he would return, was drawing near. This was 1519 in our calendar.

Now the year 1519 had come. Messengers brought reports that a band of white men had landed on the eastern coast of Mexico. They had reached a place which they named Veracruz, "True Cross," because they had arrived on Good Friday. There were more than 500 soldiers, a crew of about a hundred, some priests, workers, and Indian and Negro slaves. Sixteen horses were also taken along. Altogether there were eleven ships and a supply boat. The leader of the expedition was Captain Hernando Cortés, whom Governor Velázquez had sent with orders to trade but not to colonize.

Montezuma sent messengers to meet the strangers. The messengers brought an enormous number of treasures that were fit for the gods that he took them to be. Among these treasures were golden shields, collars of gold, beautiful shells, precious jewels and stones, necklaces, rich robes, crowns, plumes of the quetzal and other birds, and masks and mirrors used in religious ceremonies.

The messengers came on board Cortés's ship and spread the treasures before him. Cortés asked them, "Is that all? " Then he frightened them by having them tied up and firing a cannon. After that, he let them go back to the shore. In fear, they at once began the long march back as fast as they could to Tenochtitlán.

There Montezuma was waiting anxiously to hear what his messengers would report. When they returned and told what they had seen, he was filled with fear and despair. They described the noise of the cannon, the armor and weapons, and the appearance of the Spaniards. They called the horses deer, because at that time there were no horses in Mexico. The greyhounds brought by the Spaniards were also strange to the Aztecs.

Montezuma was not sure whether the strangers were really gods or only men. He sent magicians to Veracruz to work their charms against the Spaniards, but they failed. Montezuma decided to make one more effort to get the Spaniards out of Mexico.

He again sent presents to Cortés. The Spanish leader became bolder when he saw that nothing was being done to drive him away. He demanded that the Mexicans swear to obey the King of Spain, become Christians, and hand over all their gold. In addition, he insisted upon a meeting with Montezuma. The leader of the Aztecs whom Montezuma had sent to Cortés replied that Montezuma would not meet Cortés but that the Spaniards should move on. However, he said that Montezuma would send food until the Spaniards left, and that they were welcome only as visitors, if they should come back to trade.

You may wonder in what language all these conversations took place. The Aztecs and the other Indians could not speak Spanish, and the Spaniards could not speak any of the Indian languages. By a stroke of luck, Cortés found two interpreters, persons who can translate from one language into another. Each of them had a strange story.

One was a Spaniard named Jerónimo de Aguilar, who in 1511 had been on a Spanish ship that was blown off its course by the winds away from Cuba. His ship was wrecked, but he escaped in a raft and landed on Cozumel. He was picked up by Indians, whose chief took a liking to him. Aguilar mastered Mayan, the language of the Indians with whom he lived. Before Cortés landed in Veracruz, he had made some stops at nearby islands along the coast. He learned from the shouting and gestures of Indians that there was a Spaniard on Cozumel. He managed to get a message through to Aguilar, who came and sailed with Cortés. However, he spoke only Mayan of the Indian languages, not Nahuatl, the language of the Aztecs and the tribes near Veracruz.

Cortés soon found an Indian woman who could translate from Nahuatl into Mayan. Her name was Malintzin, which the Spaniards pronounced Malinche, or Malinchi. She was a princess whom her parents had given to Mayan merchants at the age of eleven, with instructions that they kill her. Instead, the merchants sold her to a chief who gave her to Cortés as a present. She was now no longer a child. She spoke both her native language, Nahuatl, and Mayan, which she learned during her wanderings with the merchants. She translated the words of Montezuma's messengers into Mayan for Aguilar, who then translated them into Spanish for Cortés.

Malinche became very devoted to the Spaniards, especially to Cortés. She was baptized and given the name Doña Marina, but is always called Malinche. She accompanied the Spaniards all through their conquest of Mexico. Soon she learned Spanish so well that Cortés no longer needed the services of Aguilar. Malinche was constantly at the side of Cortés, interpreting, giving advice, and telling the Aztecs to do what the Spaniards wished. The Aztecs began to call Cortés by the name *Malinche*, or *Malinchi*, also!

When Montezuma's representatives left, Cortés decided to go to Tenochtitlán in spite of all hardships and against the wishes of many of his soldiers. He either burned or grounded all his ships except one, which he sent to Charles V of Spain asking for permission to conquer and colonize Mexico, contrary to the orders of Velázquez. This action made him a mutineer defying the authority of his superior, the Governor of Cuba!

The distance between Veracruz and Tenochtitlán is 265 miles. Cortés and his men had to march through blazing heat, forests, swamps, deserts, mountain passes, on foot trails, or no roads at all, fighting off mosquitoes and Indians. The march took eighty-four days, from August 16 to November 8, 1519.

Cortés and his army defeated a tribe called the Tlaxcalans, who then joined them against the Aztecs, whom they hated. The Spaniards came to Cholula, where Malinche learned that the people were going to rise against the Spaniards. Cortés acted swiftly, killed off their leaders, and slaughtered the inhabitants. Then the Spaniards marched between the volcanoes Popocatépetl and Ixtaccíhuatl. Some of the soldiers climbed to the top of Popocatépetl and took sulphur from the volcano to make gunpowder.

Montezuma kept getting news about the progress of the Spaniards toward Tenochtitlán. He sent one delegation after another with more and more presents. Each group asked Cortés to go away and promised to pay him to leave. Cortés and his men had gone through too many dangers, and were too close to their goal (twenty miles away) to think of turning back. The rich presents and the gold that had been given so freely to them tempted the Spaniards to press on in spite of all dangers.

Back in his palace, Montezuma could not make up his mind whether to meet Cortés or to lead his army against him. He was still not sure whether the Spaniards were gods or their messengers. Although he was a supreme ruler looked upon almost as a god, he spent hours in discussion with his priests and nobles. His brother, Cuitlahuac, argued that once the Spaniards were allowed into Tenochtitlán, they would take Montezuma's kingdom from him. Although other nobles agreed, Montezuma said he would go out of the city to meet Cortés and invite him to enter as a guest.

On November 8, 1519, a procession of nobles marched out of Tenochtitlán in advance of Montezuma. The day was like a holiday. The people crowded the rooftops, swarmed over the lake in their canoes, and filled the streets and roads to watch the nobles go by. Montezuma was seated in a litter, a horseless carriage without wheels carried by men.

When it arrived, Montezuma got out of the litter, and four great nobles took him by the arms, helping him walk under a canopy, or covering, which was richly decorated with bright feathers, precious gems, and gold and silver designs. Four other great lords carried this canopy, while other nobles swept the ground before Montezuma, and laid coverings on the earth so that he would not soil his shoes or feet. None of the nobles except those who were holding him by the arms were allowed to look at him. His clothes were splendid; his shoes had golden soles, and jewels were set in their upper parts. The greed of the Spaniards was aroused still further; they had never before seen such splendor and richness.

Bernal Díaz, a soldier who had been on the earlier expeditions, was with Cortés during the conquest of Mexico. As an eye-witness he wrote the story of what happened. He tells how Montezuma

Montezuma

looked when he and Cortés met. The emperor was a man of about 40, slender, of good height, and well-built. His complexion was lighter than that of the other Aztecs. He had a small beard and dark hair that came down to his ears. His eyes were attractive, set in a rather long, pleasant face with a look that was sometimes warm and affectionate, sometimes sad and serious.

Montezuma brought beautiful flowers and a golden necklace of the finest workmanship for Cortés, who gave him some small gifts in return. Montezuma also presented gifts to the Spanish officers. Cortés assured Montezuma, "My men and I have come as your friends." Then Montezuma led Cortés and his followers into the city to the palace that had belonged to his father, a building so large that all the Spaniards, their horses, and their allies were able to stay in it.

Cortés and Montezuma exchanged visits. After about a week, the Spaniards began to feel almost like prisoners in the palace. Their food and water depended upon the good will of the Aztecs. The Spaniards also realized that they were so outnumbered that if Montezuma changed his mind about them, he could overpower them.

Some of the officers thought it would be a good idea to lure Montezuma into the palace and hold him prisoner. They had seen how the Aztecs looked upon him as a god, and they thought that they could use him to make the Aztecs do whatever they themselves wished. A plan of action was formed. Cortés and five officers were to visit Montezuma and quietly take him prisoner. Of course, Malinche was to go along as interpreter, and Díaz would also go with them.

Cortés sent word to Montezuma that he wished to see him. Such a request was not unusual. Montezuma replied that Cortés was welcome. Montezuma had no guards in his room. He never suspected so bold a plot against him; besides, he trusted the Spaniards. At the meeting, Cortés angrily accused Montezuma of arousing the Indians against him at Cholula, and more recently at Veracruz where they had killed a few Spanish guards. Cortés also said that Montezuma's nobles had been heard to say that their emperor wished to have the Spaniards killed.

Montezuma answered that he knew nothing about any of this. Cortés and he argued for a long time, and finally the Spanish leader said he would forgive everything if Montezuma would come quietly to the Spaniards' lodgings! If he did not go, Cortés's captains would kill him. Montezuma bravely answered that he could not be ordered about in this way and that he would not leave.

Captain Juan de Léon became very impatient. In angry tones he told Cortés that unless Montezuma agreed to go at once, he himself would stab Montezuma to death. Montezuma asked Malinche to tell him what was being said. She did, and advised him to go, or he would be killed.

Fearing for his life, Montezuma agreed to go. The Spaniards put on a friendly act, let him call his captains and a guard, and got him to say that he was going on a visit for a few days. Once in the palace where the Spaniards were staying, Montezuma was kept in a room next to Cortés. He was really a prisoner. The Spaniards allowed him to have visitors, to whom he did not tell the truth about his stay in the palace. Obeying Cortés, he did not let the nobles stir up the Aztecs against the Spaniards. He even called the chiefs of tribes together, told them to gather treasures for Cortés, and have their followers swear allegiance to the King of Spain.

Back in Cuba, Governor Velázquez learned about Cortés's march to Tenochtitlán against his orders. He sent a commander, Panfilo de Narváez, and troops to arrest Cortés and bring him back to Cuba. When Cortés learned about the landing of Narváez, he acted quickly. Leaving a garrison in charge of Pedro de Alvarado, he marched out with the rest of his troops against Narváez.

While Cortés was away, the Aztecs were permitted to celebrate the feast of their chief god, the war god Huitzilopochtli. During the wild ceremony, either because of sheer cruelty or because of a mistaken belief that the fierce actions of the Aztecs were a signal for revolt, the Spanish soldiers fired upon the crowd, killing about 3,500 of them, including 300 leaders.

The Aztecs could no longer bear to have these strangers among them. In their burning anger, they did not care whether Montezuma lived or died. The Aztec warriors assembled with their weapons. Among their leaders was Cuauhtémoc, a nephew of Montezuma. They began to attack the Spaniards inside the palace.

Meanwhile, Cortés was on his way back. He had defeated Narváez and enlisted reinforcements by persuading his men to join him, promising them gold. He also got more guns and supplies. Cortés and his men rushed back into the palace. Cortés decided to make use of Montezuma again. Unwilling at first, Montezuma finally agreed to ask the Aztecs to allow the Spaniards to leave

Tenochtitlán without attacking them. Cortés realized that his men were no longer safe in the city, and that they could be starved into surrender.

For agreeing to speak to the people, Montezuma got Cortés to allow Cuitlahuac, his brother, to leave the palace. He wanted one of the royal family to be free to become ruler if anything should happen to himself.

Montezuma went up on the roof of the palace to speak to his people. He asked them to stop fighting, to put down their arrows and shields, to avoid further bloodshed and the destruction of the city, and to let the Spaniards leave peacefully. "I am here of my own free will," he said. "I am obeying our great god, Huitzilopochtli." The crowd refused to obey Montezuma. They threw stones at him, some of which hit him. The Spaniards quickly pulled him to safety.

Shortly after this, Montezuma died. The cause of his death is not certain. Did he die of grief when he saw himself rejected by his own people? Did the stones that wounded him put an end to his life? Or, did the Spaniards, angered by Montezuma's failure to quiet the people, and by the violent resistance of the Aztecs, stab him to death? There is no absolute answer.

After the death of Montezuma, the council elected Cuitlahuac emperor. Cortés had some of the Aztecs deliver the body of Montezuma to the people outside the palace for burial. He thought that the Spaniards would gain time while the Aztecs were busy with the two ceremonies: burying Montezuma and crowning Cuitlahuac. On June 30, 1520, the Spaniards fought their way out with great slaughter on both sides. The day of that retreat is known as La Noche Triste, the Sad Night.

Looking back upon the life of Montezuma, you may wonder how he can be called a hero of Mexico. He gave in to Cortés, although he had a much larger army. He refused to yield in only one thing: he never gave up the Aztec religion for Christianity, as many other Indians did.

There is in some plays called tragedies, like those by ancient Greek writers and Shakespeare, a type of hero known as the tragic hero. He is a person of high rank like a king or great noble. He falls from his high position on account of a faulty decision, a wrong choice, caused by a weakness in his character.

Montezuma can be called a tragic hero. He was an emperor looked up to as if he were a god. He was the mightiest ruler in the western world and one of the richest men in the entire world! But he had weaknesses. He became confused, and put too much faith in myths and omens. He could not bring himself to act, but spent too much time in talking, too little in action. His people were not trained to act on their own; they looked to him for leadership. When they finally were stirred into action, it was too late.

As a tragic hero, Montezuma brought ruin upon himself and his people!

Hernando Cortés

Conqueror of Montezuma
and Cuahtémoc

5

CUAUHTÉMOC

LAST OF THE AZTEC EMPERORS

After the Spaniards left Tenochtitlán, an epidemic of smallpox broke out in the city. Among those who died from it was the ruler, Cuitlahuac. The council chose his nephew Cuauhtémoc as the emperor. He was between 25 and 30 years of age. Bernal Díaz describes him as very brave and handsome, a remarkable and distinguished-looking gentleman.

The Aztecs thought that the Spaniards would not return to Tenochtitlán. However, Cortés slowly built up his army with the help of Indians unfriendly to the Aztecs. Spanish ships came to Veracruz bringing supplies and weapons. Promising them gold and treasure, Cortés persuaded the crews to join him. He now had about 100,000 men on his side.

The Spaniards marched back to Tenochtitlán, determined to capture and destroy it, and wipe out the people, if necessary. They built ships to cross the lake and waterways, and placed cannons on the ships. The entrances to the city were so surrounded that the Aztecs found it difficult to get food. Even the aqueduct that brought fresh water from Chapultepec was cut off.

Cuauhtémoc and the Aztecs resisted with fury and bravery. They made attacks upon the Spaniards, took prisoners, sacrificed them to the god of war, and often drove the Spaniards back from places they occupied. The fighting went on for a long time. The Spaniards destroyed large sections of the city, but they lost many men. The Aztecs also suffered heavy losses, and their supply of water and food, especially meat, was running low. Some of the people were becoming discouraged and were ready to give up.

Omens were seen which further discouraged the Aztecs. They were frightened by heavy rains that lasted a whole night. A huge fire appeared in the sky. It may have been lightning, but to the superstitious Aztecs it was a sign that the place was doomed. They were losing all hope of saving their city.

Village priests and captured chiefs were sent by Cortés with messages calling upon Cuauhtémoc to surrender. When the nobles heard these messages, they spoke about the Spaniards' greed for gold, their plundering of the cities, the enslavement of the people, and the misery they had brought to the land. They all felt, "It is better to die while fighting than to become slaves of those who will mistreat and torture us for gold." Cuauhtémoc then threatened death to anybody who dared talk about peace and surrender.

When the Aztecs refused to surrender, Cortés sent his men and ships into action. After a week of bitter fighting, the Spaniards reached the palace of Cuauhtémoc. They were under orders to bring him back unharmed. Cuauhtémoc and a few men were in a small boat, part of a fleet battling with the larger Spanish ships. He was quickly recognized and tried to escape, but the Spaniards captured him.

Cuauhtémoc was taken directly to Cortés, who had prepared a royal welcome for him. He looked upon him as a foe worthy of respect because of his heroism and courage. When Cuauhtémoc saw the sword or dagger hanging in Cortés's belt, he said to his conqueror that he had fought as long as he could for his people but now that it was all over, "I am your prisoner; it is better that you take that knife and kill me at once." However, Cortés embraced him, telling him that he had nothing to fear. He promised Cuauhtémoc that he would remain as ruler of his people, and that no harm would come to him.

Where this meeting took place there now stands a church bearing an inscription in Spanish, "This is the place where slavery began. Here the emperor was taken prisoner on the afternoon of the 13th of August, 1521."

Torture of Cuauhtémoc

Actually, Cortés was keeping Cuauhtémoc as a hostage, just as he had kept Montezuma, to have a hold over the Aztecs. Cortés soon forgot part of his promise, and in less than four years he broke it entirely.

Love of gold proved to be stronger than any promise made to a beaten enemy. The Spaniards demanded that the Aztecs bring them all the gold that they had. Although the Aztecs brought loads of gold bars, plates, crowns, and ornaments in their canoes, the Spaniards were still not satisfied.

They were told that Cuauhtémoc knew where more was. All he could tell them was that there was more in the lake. Therefore, Cortés ordered him and a noble to be tortured. Red-hot irons were placed against the soles of their feet. Cuauhtémoc bore the pain bravely without uttering a cry. As his companion moaned and shrieked, Cuauhtémoc said to him, "Do not think that I am enjoying this foot-bath of fire, just because I am not screaming out with pain." When no information could be gotten out of them, Cortés ordered the torture to be stopped.

Cuauhtémoc bore the scars of the heated irons for the rest of his life. Near the end of the year 1524, he was forced by Cortés to go with him and his army toward Honduras, far to the south of Mexico. In addition, more than 3,000 Aztec soldiers had to go along. Cortés was afraid to leave Cuauhtémoc behind with so many Aztec warriors, thinking they might revolt.

The march through the jungle was long and terrible. Hunger, constant rain, and snakes brought horror to Cortés's mind, until he became almost insane. He seemed to hear rumors that the Aztecs were planning to kill the Spaniards, return to Tenochtitlán, and drive the Spaniards out of Mexico.

He called Cuauhtémoc before him and questioned him. The Aztec emperor said that he had no such plans or intentions. In spite of his denial, Cortés placed him and his cousin on trial. He judged them both guilty of treason. There was no proof, but Cortés was too mad to listen to reason. Both Cuauhtémoc and his cousin were hanged on February 28, 1525.

Bernal Díaz reported the trial and execution. He wrote that the Spanish soldiers were deeply shocked and ashamed, and that they considered the sentence wrong and unjust.

Cuauhtémoc was as noble and brave in death as he had been in life. He said to Cortés when he learned what his fate was going to be, "I have always known how untruthful you were, Malinchi. I am happy to die, but you should have killed me when I surrendered to you. You will be punished by God."

So died the last emperor of the Aztecs, Mexico's first great military and national hero. The scene of his torture has been the subject of paintings and murals; his face appears on coins and stamps. There is a huge bronze statue of Cuauhtémoc at the crossing of two important avenues in Mexico City. Around the base are scenes of events in his life; above it are the names of Cuitlahuac and other Aztec leaders. Every August 13, on the anniversary of his capture and the taking of Tenochtitlán by the Spaniards, a ceremony begins around the statue, ending with Indian dances on the 21st.

As you have read of the downfall of Montezuma and Cuauhtémoc, you may have wondered how the Aztecs lost to a few hundred Spaniards. The Aztecs had many more fighters, good weapons and armor, and were on their home ground. Once they learned that the Spaniards were not gods, the Aztecs could see that they could be beaten.

The Aztecs did not know how to take advantage of their superior numbers. Not all of them could take part in the fighting at one time. They did not split the Spaniards and their allies into smaller units and wipe them out one group at a time.

When the Aztecs had victory in their grasp, they let the Spaniards get away, as on the Sad Night. They stopped to take prisoners back for sacrifices, and they halted to strip the bodies of the dead for plunder.

The Aztecs failed to make the conquered tribes a part of their own nation. The result was that the tribes hated them, and were ready to join the Spaniards against them.

The Aztecs had a caste system, a society with different levels. The lowest members could not rise and were trained to obey their leaders. When these leaders were killed off or captured, the ordinary soldiers were helpless.

With the death of Cuauhtémoc, the line of emperors came to an end. Tenochtitlán was totally destroyed; a new Spanish city rose in its place, now known as Mexico City.

6

SOR JUANA INÉS DE LA CRUZ

THE LITERARY NUN

Until modern times there were no careers open to women in Mexico. Rarely did a woman do anything unusual publicly, as did Catalina de Erazu in the early 1600's. She dressed herself as a man and became famous as a swordsman and bandit of three countries: Peru, Chile, and Mexico.

In her time a Mexican woman might get a position in the court of the Viceroy to wait on his wife, or enter a convent to become a nun. One young lady of genius did both, besides becoming one of Mexico's greatest writers.

Her name was Juana Inés de Asbaje y Ramirez Santillana. She was born on November 12, 1651 in a farmhouse in the village of San Miguel Nepantla near Mexico City.

Juana was a very bright child who was eager to learn. One day, when she was only three years old, she followed her sister, who was going to the house of a friend of the family to be taught. Little Juana listened to the lesson excitedly and wanted to learn to read, too. She told the teacher that her mother had also sent her for a lesson.

She was a fast learner. In two years she was able to read, write, count, and do fine sewing. She began to write poetry. Before she was eight, she wrote a poem for a religious festival. Juana wanted to learn more than anybody in the small village could teach her. She read all the books she could put her hands on, especially her grandfather's.

Sor Juana Inés de la Cruz

When she was eight years old, the family moved to Mexico City. She took lessons in Latin, in which she excelled after only twenty lessons. She was so anxious to learn that she made up a schedule for herself. She cut her hair. If it grew back before she learned the subject she was studying, she cut it again. She stopped cutting her hair only when she had mastered the subject! She wrote that a head without anything in it should not be covered with anything so beautiful as hair.

She grew up to be a lovely young lady. Her reputation for beauty and intelligence spread throughout Mexico City. She was invited to live in the Viceroy's palace as lady-in-waiting to his wife. One day the Viceroy called scholars and professors of the University of Mexico to the palace. They asked Juana all kinds of questions, as in an examination. She passed with high honors.

Juana was almost sixteen at that time. Suddenly, she decided to become a nun. She wrote that she wanted to live quietly and peacefully away from the busy world so she could study. On August 14, 1667 she entered a convent. Her name now became Sor Juana Inés de la Cruz (Sister Juana Inés of the Cross). After a few months she became very ill and left. However, more than a year later, on November 24, 1669, she entered the convent of San Jerónimo, where she remained for the rest of her life.

She took with her a large number of books, musical and scientific instruments, and maps. She was unable to live the peaceful life that she wanted because many visitors came to see her, and she had to write plays for festivals and answer many letters.

She also wrote books, some of which did not please the heads of the church. She became ill, and the doctors told her not to work so hard. The Mother Superior ordered her not to study. Sister Juana Inés found it so unbearable to live without her books that she was allowed to return to them.

Her strong will, her independent mind, and her love of books and learning soon got her into trouble. She disagreed with some ideas that a famous priest, Father Vieira, used in a sermon. Her disagreement was reported to the Bishop of Puebla, who wrote her a letter which he signed with the name Sor Filotea. In it he ordered her to give up her books, and to devote herself only to religion.

Sister Juana answered this letter. She wrote about her life, her ideas, and her reasons for wanting to learn from books and to write books herself, pointing out that even the Saints loved books of all kinds. She defended her right to disagree with Father Vieira's sermon, and wrote that she favored education for women, who should not be asked to obey men without question! From this answer we learn much about her life.

However, she did not win. She was ordered to give up her books and to lead a strict religious life. She disposed of her 4,000 books, (except for a few holy ones), her maps, and her musical and scientific instruments, and devoted herself entirely to religion.

Two years later an epidemic hit Mexico City. Many of the sisters in the convent became ill. Sister Juana nursed them until she herself caught the illness. She died, at almost 44, on April 17, 1695.

Different volumes of selections from her poems were published over the years, but until recently there was no complete collection of her works. These fill four volumes, published in Mexico City between 1951 and 1957.

Sor Juana Inés de la Cruz wrote plays, including a comedy. She also wrote a few prose pieces, like the answer to the Bishop's letter. Most of her work is lyric poetry, which means poetry that can be put to music. Her love of poetry is filled with tenderness and deep feeling, and her religious poetry is beautiful and pure.

Critics have called her one of the greatest poets of the Spanish language. One, Miguel Ángel Menéndez y Pelayo, says that her love poems "are the most gentle and delicate that have ever come from the pen of a woman." Her poems of this type have such deep feeling and sound so true that it is believed that Juana went into a convent because she was disappointed in love.

In the ancient Greek myths there are nine Muses, goddesses of the arts, like poetry, music, and the dance. When a woman became a great poet, she was sometimes called the Tenth Muse. In the title of Sor Juana's first volume of poems published in Madrid, Spain, in 1689, while she was still alive, she was called "the Unique Poetess, the Tenth Muse."

She brought glory not only to Mexico, but to all women!

7

FATHER HIDALGO

THE FATHER OF MEXICAN INDEPENDENCE

Every year, on the night of September 15, a large crowd gathers in front of the National Palace in Mexico City. Above the center of the main entrance is a very famous old church bell. Once it was in a church in the village of Nuestra Señora de Dolores (Our Lady of Sorrows), or simply Dolores, which was renamed Dolores Hidalgo in 1826.

This is the Liberty Bell of Mexico. A village priest named Father Hidalgo once rang it to call the people together to rise up against the Spaniards. At eleven o'clock the bell begins to ring. The President of Mexico (or his representative) cries out, *"Mexicanos, Viva Méjico"* ("Mexicans, Long live Mexico"), the beginning of the speech by which Father Hidalgo aroused the people on September 16, 1810, Mexico's Independence Day. The people packing the plaza around the Palace join in with the same shout.

Hidalgo's cry is known as *El Grito de Dolores*, "The Cry of Dolores." It marked the beginning of the eleven-year struggle of the Mexican people for independence from Spanish rule.

Miguel Hidalgo (full name Miguel Hidalgo y Costilla) was born on May 8, 1753 in San Vicente del Caño, in the state of Guanajuato. His father was a Creole, a Spaniard born in Mexico, who worked as manager of an hacienda, or large farm. The name *Hidalgo* has a special meaning in Spanish, "son of somebody," a noble. It may mean that the family was once of noble rank. Miguel's mother came from one of the best-known Spanish families of Mexico.

His first teacher was his father, from whom he learned to read and write. The Indians spoke to him about their problems and work on the farm. At fourteen, he went to Colegio San Nicolás (St. Nicholas College) in Valladolid. This building is still standing, and from its records we have learned much about Hidalgo. The word *College* in the name of this school means that it also prepares the students to go to what we call a college.

At first young Hidalgo wanted to study agriculture, but he showed such ability in other subjects that he decided to become a priest. After three years, when he was only seventeen, Miguel was able to pass the examinations of the University of Mexico for the degree of Bachelor of Arts, which he received on March 30, 1770. Continuing his studies, in May 1773, he became a Bachelor of Arts in theology, the study of religion. He went back to San Nicolás to teach Latin, philosophy, and theology. While teaching, he won a prize for two papers on theology, one written in Spanish, the other in Latin.

Soon after this he became a priest, but he remained in the College. There he became the treasurer, and later the rector or principal. He made changes in the courses of study that were not popular with some of the other teachers and priests. As a result, on February 2, 1792, Hidalgo left the college and took up a position as a *cura*, or village priest, in San Felipe where he stayed for eleven years. By talking against the teachings of the Catholic Church, he got into trouble, but he recanted, or took back what he said.

In 1803 he became the village priest of Nuestra Señora de Dolores. He led a very active life, discussing books with friends and helping to change the way of life of the village. He had the Indians plant mulberry trees to get silk from cocoons spun by silkworms that feed on the leaves. Because the Spanish government ruling Mexico did not allow silk to be produced there, officers came and destroyed the trees. Hidalgo then built small factories to give work to the Indians. Some of the articles made by them became so famous that visitors came from far places to buy the leather goods and pottery. Pottery is still made in Dolores Hidalgo.

Hidalgo made many enemies because of his ideas and teachings, and what he was doing for the Indians. Many of the Spaniards and even some of the Creoles did not want the Indians to advance. They preferred to keep the Indians as workers receiving low wages. Hidalgo's enemies tried to get him into trouble with the Church, but they failed, and he continued to help the Indians. By learning a number of their languages, he could speak to them in their own dialects. He listened to their complaints, and was respected and loved by the Indians.

Things went on in this way until the revolution broke out in September 1810. Hidalgo was then more than 47 years old, of medium height and dark complexion with green eyes. He was

partly bald and seemed a little bent over because his shoulders were stooped. He did not look like a man who would lead a revolution.

At this point we must look at what was happening in Mexico and its ruling country, Spain. Napoleon had conquered Spain and made King Ferdinand VII a prisoner. Many Mexicans thought it was a good time to try to gain independence from Spain, as it could no longer be considered a free country.

In Mexico itself there was a great need of reforms to better the conditions of the people. The population of less than six million was made up of four different groups. The smallest group (about 15,000) was the Spaniards. They were called Europeans, and came from Spain. There were about 600,000 Creoles. They were called Americans, and were Spaniards born in America. There were almost 1,500,000 mestizos, or half-breeds, descendants of Spaniards and Indians, and more than 3,500,000 Indians. In addition, there was a very small number of Negroes, together with some mulattoes of Negro-Indian or Negro-Spanish parentage called zambos.

The Spaniards looked down upon all the other groups, with no exceptions. The Spaniards were the merchants and capitalists. They held the highest government and church positions, and most of the leading positions in the army. Many Creoles were landlords. Some mestizos were either skilled workers or ordinary laborers. The Indians were the lowest class, working in the fields or on land held in common. Many of them were peons, the lowest paid workers on farms, like serfs, or slaves.

In addition, Spain made life hard for all the inhabitants. The Inquisition, a branch of the Catholic Church that punished heretics, those who worked against the teachings of the Church, was in power in Mexico. The Inquisition did not allow certain books to be read, and severely punished anyone caught reading them. The government put heavy taxes on almost everything a person could buy. It did not allow coffee and olives to be planted or silk to be produced. Foreign ships were forbidden to enter Mexican ports as Spain wanted complete control of sending goods to Mexico so that her own merchants could make all the profits.

Living was so hard for so many of the inhabitants of Mexico that they were ready for a revolution. Excited by the American and French Revolutions and by the spirit of revolt in Spain against Napoleon, many were ready for action.

Many Creoles and almost all the mestizos sympathized with the miseries of the Indians. As a boy and village priest, Hidalgo had learned about these at first-hand. He himself had almost been a victim of the Inquisition at San Felipe and Dolores. By reading forbidden books, and by his reforms and ideas, he angered those who wanted the old ways kept. Hidalgo and his friends desired a new life for all Mexicans with the Spaniards driven out of the country.

Ignacio de Allende

The first move toward a new life came from a friend of Hidalgo, Captain Ignacio de Allende, who realized that as a Creole he might not rise any higher in the army, and he was ambitious. Conditions in Mexico deeply moved him. He formed a club ("Society for the Study of Fine Arts") whose members were important and educated Creoles. They were supposed to discuss books but instead they talked about revolution when they met at Querétaro, not far from Dolores.

Hidalgo soon became the leader of the club. A revolution was planned with Allende as its commander-in-chief. Believing that most of the people would not want to declare themselves openly against the King of Spain, the members of the club decided only to drive out the Spaniards and take away their property. As members sought supporters, Hidalgo was chosen to get the help of village priests. These, in turn, were to ask their congregations to join in the revolution.

December 8, 1810, was picked as the date because this was the day of a great fair with much excitement and large crowds. Unfortunately, word of the plot got to the government officials. A few of the conspirators were arrested. Allende was visiting Hidalgo in Dolores. Miguel Domínguez, Mayor of Querétaro, was ordered to seize the conspirators in his city.

The Mayor and his wife were secretly on the side of the conspirators. He pretended to make the arrests, while his wife sent a warning to Captain Juan Aldama, Captain Allende's chief assistant, through the town jailer, Ignacio Pérez. Aldama and Pérez raced on horseback to Dolores to give the warning. They are called the Paul Reveres of the Mexican Revolution. Long before dawn on September 16, 1810, they arrived at Dolores. (A few writers believe this happened on the 15th.)

Hidalgo received the news calmly. Calling his followers together, he explained what had happened. They wanted to escape, but Hidalgo said, "Gentlemen, we are lost. The only thing we can do is seize the gachupines." *Gachupines* means those who wear spurs; it was a term used by the Mexicans to show their contempt for the Spaniards.

The conspirators first opened the jails and set the prisoners free. Then, with their help, they seized the Spaniards in Dolores, about twenty in all. The people were gathering at the church for an early mass. Father Hidalgo appeared in his everyday clothes. The church bell rang. From the steps of the church, Father Hidalgo addressed the huge crowd that grew larger as the bell kept ringing. He told them to overthrow the Spaniards and take back the land they had stolen. He urged the crowd to follow him. Shouting "Death to the gachupines! Long live Mexico!" they were ready to do whatever he asked.

Some of the men armed themselves with whatever weapons they could find: shovels, clubs, farm tools and old guns. Father Hidalgo's band of about one hundred men were workers: servants, farmhands, cowboys, laborers, gardeners, and carpenters. Arriving at the nearby village of Atotonilco, Father Hidalgo took a picture of the Virgin of Guadalupe, the patron saint of Mexico, from the church. Holding it high for all to see, he called it the emblem of the army and of their cause. They called themselves Los Insurgentes, the Insurgents, those who rise up.

Church of Dolores

Under the leadership of Hidalgo and Allende, the Insurgents won victory after victory. More and more Indian slaves and peons ran away from their masters to join them; mestizos and Creoles came as volunteers. Additional leaders, like Father Morelos, raised bands of fighters in other parts of Mexico.

The army of Hidalgo and Allende defeated the Royalists at Celaya. *Royalists* was the name given to the Viceroy's soldiers. Then the Insurgents attacked Guanajuato, a mining town, rich in silver and gold, and noted for its opals. Then, as now, conditions were very bad for the miners, mostly mestizos, and a few Indians. Many of them had joined the Insurgents.

In Guanajuato there was a huge stone building that was used for storage, called the Alhóndiga de Granaditas. To the miners it

53

represented the Government; it was strong, hard, and powerful. The Royalist troops were holding it as a fortress. The Insurgents looked upon it as something that had to be stormed and taken, just as the citizens of Paris felt about the Bastille at the beginning of the French Revolution on July 14, 1789!

One brave Insurgent, an Indian miner named José Barajas, managed to get his comrades into the fortress. A large stone slab was put on his back, and he made his way to the heavy door of the fort. This he smeared with tar and oil, and then set it on fire. Soon the Insurgents were able to get through this opening. They lost hundreds of men as they battled their way in, because the Royalists fought back bravely. However, in the end the Royalists were slaughtered. The Insurgents nicknamed the brave soldier Pípila, which means Turkey, because he had a long neck. Today there is a large statue of Pípila high up on a hill overlooking the main square of Guanajuato!

Hidalgo was promoted by the leaders of the Revolution and given the title Captain General. Allende was also promoted and was named Lieutenant General. After the successes of the Insurgents, they seemed ready to march on Mexico City. First, Hidalgo stopped at Valladolid for two days. There he met a Creole who had military experience. He was Agustín de Iturbide. Hidalgo offered him a high position because he was anxious to have experienced military men, especially Creoles, in his army. Iturbide refused and later joined the Royalists.

At Valladolid, Hidalgo received a warning and advice that he did not follow. A sergeant-major advised him to pick and train about 15,000 men. "Otherwise," he warned Hidalgo, "after the first defeat you will be left alone. They will run away like frightened rabbits."

Hidalgo's army consisted mainly of Indians, runaway slaves, and peons. They were untrained and hard to discipline. When they took a city, they ran wild, broke into houses, took what they could, and burned what they could not sell. They broke machinery and set fire to the mines. When they lost a battle, or when things were not going well, they went into a panic.

Many of Hidalgo's officers, including Allende, were against such behavior. They also did not want a complete revolution; all they wanted was a change of government. Many Creoles who owned land did not want to lose their possessions, and so they even opposed Hidalgo. He was making great changes in the districts that he controlled by ordering slaves to be set free, and doing away with many taxes, especially those that the Indians and mestizos had to pay to the Spaniards. Another rule he made was that only the Indians could cultivate the land owned by them. The Catholic Church of Mexico opposed Hidalgo because it owned much land.

In spite of the forces against them, Hidalgo and his followers were very successful at the beginning, and it looked as if the Viceroy's government would fall. The Insurgent army marched to Mexico City and took up a position only twelve miles away.

Hidalgo was now the Generalissimo, or supreme commander, of the Insurgent army. Allende and a few other generals opposed his strategy, but he was too popular to be overruled. Hidalgo generally wore a plain uniform, but as Generalissimo he wore a brilliant uniform, a blue coat with red cuffs and collar embroidered with gold and silver. He always wore a gold medal with the image of the Virgin of Guadalupe as the protector of the Revolution.

The spirit of the army was very high. From a small band they had increased to more than 100,000, with plenty of money to carry on a war. Their funds came from money taken away from the Royalists, Spaniards, and the Church. They also took ammunition and supplies from the Royalists.

For some reason Hidalgo did not order an attack upon Mexico City. He never told why, but it is believed that he shuddered when he thought of what might happen if his men were let loose there. Perhaps he recalled how they had murdered and robbed in other cities, and feared they might become an uncontrolled and undisciplined mob that could be slaughtered by the Viceroy's trained soldiers.

He gave orders to turn about and head back to Querétaro. Many of his men began to leave the army while the Royalist forces grew larger. Hidalgo's army suffered a defeat. He rallied his men and marched to Guadalajara.

Meanwhile, the Royalists had sent their ablest and most determined general, Félix María Calleja, toward Guadalajara. Against the advice of Allende, Hidalgo decided to meet Calleja at Calderón Bridge, not far from Guadalajara. There, on January 17, 1811, the two armies met in a fierce battle that went on for six hours. The Insurgents were on the point of victory when an accident took place that delayed the independence of Mexico for ten years. A shell blew up one of the Insurgents' ammunition wagons. The Insurgents went into a panic and ran in all directions.

The sergeant-major's warning at Valladolid had come true!

Hidalgo had to give up what was left of the army to Allende. As Calleja kept pursuing the Insurgents in the area, Allende tried to lead a group of about 1,000 towards Texas, then a part of Mexico. They were ambushed, captured, and taken under heavy guard to Chihuahua, where Allende, Aldama, and another officer, José Mariano Jiménez, were quickly tried for fighting the government by a military court and executed by a firing squad. Hidalgo was tried by the Church also, since he was a priest, and after the Church had declared him no longer a priest, he was turned over to the army for execution.

Then he was sentenced to be shot on the morning of July 30, 1811. He faced his last hours with courage and even humor. When asked whether he had anything to say, he answered, "Yes, get me some candy for the firing squad." When his last breakfast was being brought to him, he saw that the bowl was not filled with milk. He asked, "Because this is the last, does it have to be the least? " Finally, when he was led to the place of execution, he remembered that he had left the candy under his pillow. He asked a soldier to run back for it, and then handed it out. When the firing squad was getting ready, he placed his hand over his heart to show the soldiers where to shoot.

The heads of Hidalgo and the three officers were hung in iron cages on the four corners of the Alhóndiga in Guanajuato, and were not taken down until 1821, when Mexico won its independence from Spain. Their bodies and heads were buried in tombs in Mexico City. More than a hundred years later, all four, Hidalgo, Aldama, Allende, and Jiménez, were moved with other heroes of the War of Independence to their final resting place beneath the Monument of Independence in Mexico City. There an eternal flame burns as a reminder of the spirit of liberty that cannot be put out!

Other honors have been given to Hidalgo and the officers who died with him. Many places have been named after them. The name of the city from which Allende came, San Miguel el Grande, was changed to San Miguel de Allende. His home there is marked with a historic tablet. The pictures of some of them are on stamps and money.

Hidalgo has been honored in the work of Mexican artists. A great mural by Orozco in the Governor's Palace in Guadalajara, where Hidalgo signed the document freeing the slaves, shows him holding that paper.

Mural of Hidalgo by Orozco

Hidalgo's reforms began something that others have carried forward. The fight that he, Allende, and Aldama started, and for which they and others gave their lives, ended in freedom for Mexico. As the first great leader in that fight, Hidalgo is called "The Father of the Fatherland" and "The Father of Mexican Independence."

8

JOSEFA ORTIZ DE DOMÍNGUEZ

A BRAVE WOMAN IN THE FIGHT FOR INDEPENDENCE

The Mexicans call her La Corregidora, which means the Mayor's Wife. Her serious, stern face looks up at you from a five-centavo piece called a *Josefina*, or from a twenty-peso bill.

Her full name is María Josefa Ortiz de Domínguez. She was born in Mexico City in 1773 (records differ; some say Valladolid in 1768). Left an orphan at an early age, she was taken care of by her sister. Shortly after completing her education in 1791, she married Don Miguel Domínguez, a native of Mexico City, where he was born in 1756. He was active in the Viceroy's service, and soon after the marriage, he was appointed Mayor of Querétaro.

There she became friendly with Captain Allende, who was in love with her daughter. He confided some of the plans of the conspirators to Señora de Domínguez, who was sympathetic to the cause of independence and won her husband over. Learning where the weapons of the garrison were kept, she managed to get some of them to the conspirators.

When the Mayor was ordered to arrest the conspirators, he locked his wife up in her room so that she might not carelessly

La Corregidora

talk to anybody who was under suspicion. Señora de Domínguez, however, got word to the jailer, Ignacio Pérez, whose room was directly under hers, by tapping on the floor to attract his attention.

The building in which the Mayor and his wife lived was a government building, like a city hall. It is still standing and is now the Palacio Municipal, the Municipal Building, of Querétaro. From the balcony of her room, The Cry of Dolores is recited on the night of September 15, as in Mexico City and Dolores Hidalgo.

Pérez came up to find out what the tapping meant. He spoke to Señora de Domínguez through the large keyhole of the lock. She whispered to him what she wanted him to do. The ride to Hidalgo at Dolores followed.

In spite of all the precautions that had been taken, an informer was suspicious and placed charges against Señora de Domínguez, who was arrested. She was placed in a convent as a prisoner but was released for a time because she was bearing a child. Then she was sent to another convent in Mexico City where she remained for three years.

House of La Corregidora

Her husband came to Mexico City to defend her. When a new Viceroy granted amnesty after the death of Morelos in 1815, she was set free. Don Miguel and his wife lost all their property, which was never returned to them.

Doña Josefa de Domínguez was a woman of strong will and great courage. She dared to speak up to Hidalgo against the massacre of the Royalists when his men captured the Alhóndiga. During her imprisonment she showed great firmness and scolded her jailers. After Iturbide became Emperor in 1822, he thought he was honoring her by offering her a position in the Court as lady-in-waiting to his wife, the Empress. She firmly refused, since her dream of a free Mexico did not foresee it as an Empire! She

Lock with keyhole through which La Corregidora
talked to the jailer (Regional Museum, Querétaro)

showed her independence by objecting to the expulsion of
Spaniards from Mexico by President Guadalupe Victoria.

Don Miguel took an active part in the government after the
expulsion of Iturbide. He ended his career as President of the
Supreme Court, a position he held until his death in 1830. Doña
Josefa had died the year before. Mexico has not forgotten her. Her
picture appears not only on coins and paper money but also on
stamps. In a pleasant little square in Mexico City, there is a bronze
statue of La Corregidora. Finally, as a heroine who was devoted to
Mexican independence, she has been given a title of merit and
honor for distinguished service: *Benemérita de la Patria*, "Well-
Deserving of the Country."

9

JOSÉ MORELOS

HUMBLE SERVANT OF THE NATION

Morelia, capital of the state of Michoacán, is a beautiful city
west of Mexico City. It was founded in 1541 by Don Antonio de
Mendoza, the first viceroy, who called it Valladolid from the name
of his home city in Spain. In 1829, the Mexican people renamed it
Morelia in honor of one of their greatest fighters for independence, José María Morelos y Pavón, who was born there on
September 30, 1765.

José was the son of a poor carpenter, Manuel Morelos, and a
remarkable woman, Juana María Pérez Pavón, who was well-
educated. Their son was considered a mestizo, because the father
was probably part Indian, and his mother a Creole. José's parents
were poor. Since there were two other children, a boy and a girl,
young José went to work to help the family. His mother, a
schoolteacher's daughter, taught the boy how to read and write.

His father died in 1779, when José was fourteen years old. The
boy was sent to an uncle, who was the owner of an hacienda, or
large plantation or farm. There José started as a laborer, then
drove a mule train which carried silk brought from the Far East to
Acapulco, a large port on the western coast of Mexico. Mule trains

took the silk from there to Mexico City. The Mexico City-Acapulco road was called the China Road because goods to or from China and the Orient were carried on this road. On the way José studied whenever he could, often from books he bought in Mexico City. Traveling back and forth on the roads, he became familiar with the country in which he would one day fight many battles.

While José was working on his uncle's farm, his mother had great hopes that he would become a priest. There was a chance that he would inherit some property from her grandfather, but only if he became a priest. With this property and with a steady income, no matter how small, he could take better care of his mother and family. For these reasons, and because his mother had great influence over him, he decided to follow her wishes.

First he had to prepare himself by taking regular courses of study, including Latin. In 1790, when he was 25 years old, he entered San Nicolás College in Valladolid, where Father Hidalgo was the rector. Morelos was a model student. His grammar teacher wrote, "He has raised himself above all other students."

In 1792, Morelos transferred to another school in Morelia to take a required Latin course and others not being given at San Nicolás. He again led the class, and in March 1795, went to Mexico City to take the examinations for the degree of Bachelor of Arts at the University. He passed them, and was given the degree on April 28, 1795.

While preparing to become a priest, he taught for a year in Uruapan. On December 18, 1797, he was appointed a priest by the Bishop of Michoacán and assigned to Uruapan and its neighborhood.

Like Father Hidalgo, he was a *cura,* or village priest. The village priests were the hardest working and poorest paid of all the priests in Mexico. They were sent to remote villages inhabited by poor Indians who had to pay a special tax to support them. It is easy to see why many village priests joined the revolt against Spanish rule.

After a short stay in the city of Uruapan, Morelos was suddenly sent to the small village of Churumuco on January 31, 1798. His mother and sister went to live with him there. All three suffered in the hot climate. When his mother became ill, she had to be rushed back toward Valladolid. On January 5, 1799, she died before she could reach it. The news did not get to Morelos for some time.

Before he learned of his mother's death, Morelos wrote to his bishop, asking for a change to a cooler place. He mentioned that his mother had become ill from the heat and that he did not think she would recover. After a few months the bishop transferred him to Carácuaro, a village not far from Churumuco. This was a change without a difference. The climate was almost the same. Morelos was disappointed, but he obeyed without complaining. The news of his mother's death had come as a bitter blow to him. She had been a great influence in his life and had brought him comfort, love, and devotion.

He remained in Carácuaro for eleven years. There he led a poor and unexciting life. The Indians often couldn't pay the taxes for his salary. He raised cows and goats and sold them in Valladolid. His life changed after Father Hidalgo uttered the Cry of Dolores on September 16, 1810. When Hidalgo was fighting near Valladolid, Morelos got a leave of absence to see him. He remembered that Hidalgo had been the rector of San Nicolás when he himself was a student there about twenty years before. Morelos wanted to learn more about what was going on.

On October 20, 1810, they met in the village of Indaparapeo, and a historic conversation took place between the two village priests. The talk lasted for several hours, and Hidalgo convinced Morelos of the justice of his cause. When Morelos asked to be made a chaplain in the Insurgents' army, Hidalgo answered that he would make a better officer than a chaplain, and wrote out a commission appointing Morelos a lieutenant. He also gave him a number of very difficult tasks. Morelos was asked to raise an army, collect weapons and ammunition, capture all Spaniards and deport their families, take away their property, seize Acapulco, and reorganize the government in the places taken.

Morelos began almost immediately to carry out Hidalgo's instructions. He rounded up an army of about 2,000 recruits, and captured a large number of towns and cities, failing only to take Acapulco. In the captured places his men took a great supply of cannons and ammunition.

Morelos seemed to know exactly what to do as a commander, although he had lived as a student and priest. One secret of his success was that, unlike Hidalgo, he chose a small group of tough, well-disciplined fighters, was very strict, and trained his men well. He spent months in some of the captured places training his men before marching on. Cowardice, disobedience, and treachery were severely punished. In addition, he picked good officers who did not fight each other for their own selfish interests.

Although both sides slaughtered prisoners and even inhabitants of places they captured, Morelos or his officers sometimes showed a more humane policy that won men over to his side. Two incidents will illustrate this policy.

Two men had been sent by the Royalists from Mexico City to kill Morelos. Word about the plot got to him from a priest in Mexico City. The two men were arrested when they came to the army. Instead of having them put to death, as they expected, Morelos treated them kindly. In return, they became his supporters and fought for liberty.

The other incident concerns one of his officers, a young man named Nicolás Bravo. He joined Morelos together with his father, Leonardo, and three uncles. His father had been captured by the Royalists and sentenced to death. The Viceroy offered to spare his life if Nicolás would accept amnesty and stop fighting. Nicolás refused because he did not want to weaken the cause of Morelos. Morelos offered 800 prisoners in exchange for Leonardo, but the Viceroy put Leonardo to death.

Morelos then ordered Nicolás to put to death 300 Royalist prisoners held by him. Instead, Nicolás made a speech to them in which he told them about the offer to the Viceroy, the execution of his father, and the orders given to him. He asked them, "How can you serve such a vile master like your Viceroy, who might have saved all of you and would not, just for the sake of one life—my father's? But I am not the Viceroy. Go, you are free! You may go wherever you wish."

The prisoners were amazed at such words, and remained, shouting: "We are not going! We will remain to fight for the independence of Mexico with you! Long live our General! "

Four of them who wanted to go back into private life were allowed to leave in safety, and the others became a part of Morelos's army!

In February 1812, after a number of victories by his own army and by some of his generals, Morelos took up his position in Cuautla. There his army was attacked by General Calleja, and after a brilliant defense lasting seventy-two days, the Insurgents had to retreat from the city because of lack of water and food. Calleja thought that the loss of Cuautla meant the end of the war.

Morelos was far from being beaten. With a smaller force, he had held back the Royalists for more than two months, giving time to Insurgent leaders elsewhere to raise new armies. At this time

Calleja sent a message to Morelos from the Viceroy offering him amnesty if he would stop fighting. Morelos refused the pardon offered to him, and answered, "I offer the same favor to Calleja and his men."

The Insurgent armies were now successful almost everywhere, winning victories and capturing cities and towns. Morelos took the large cities of Oaxaca and Acapulco. He had reached the height of his fame and was the most successful leader among the Insurgents.

At the time of the capture of Acapulco in 1813, he was 48 years old. His looks were not imposing, as he was only a little

José María Morelos

more than five feet in height. He had a large scar across his nose, and his dark face was marked by warts. He had brown eyes and thick lips. Because he suffered from severe headaches, he constantly wore a handkerchief around his head.

Morelos had also been carrying out another of Hidalgo's orders—to reorganize the government of the land he occupied. However, both he and other Insurgent leaders felt that there should be a central government of the Insurgents with authority over all the leaders. This government would work out solutions of the problems that faced all of them. Under the leadership of Morelos, delegates were appointed to meet at Chilpancingo.

The Congress of Chilpancingo, as the group is called, met on September 8, 1813. Morelos was appointed commander-in-chief, Generalissimo, of the Insurgent army. However, he preferred a title that sounded less grand. In a speech to the Congress, he said:

"I do not seek the presidency. My work will cease once the junta is established. I shall consider myself much honored with the title of Humble Servant of the Nation."

The Congress issued a Declaration of Independence, and on November 6, 1813, added another document which has been called Mexico's First Constitution. For the most part, this contains Morelos's ideas on social reforms and changes in Mexico.

Morelos had carried out a few of these reforms before. He had declared them to the people and also to the officers so that they

Stamps honoring the First Constitution

68

would know what he was fighting for. His own motto was, "Independence, a democratic republic, and distribution of land." The Constitution declared: (1) that there would be no more slavery (2) that Mexico was free and independent (3) that there would be no more castes, but that all Mexicans would be equal (4) that Spaniards would be deported (5) that the Catholic religion was the official religion of Mexico (6) that government monopolies, absolute control and ownership of any industry by the government, were to be broken up (7) that there should be a 5% income tax and a 10% import tax on foreign goods brought into Mexico.

All Church lands would be seized as well as the haciendas of the rich Creoles and Spaniards. The land taken would then be split up into small pieces and given to the peasants. The Constitution made provisions for voting, elections, a supreme court, and a congress. The Mexicans were now known as the Americans, but the Spaniards were called the Europeans. The new motto was, "America for the Americans! " The rich Creoles, the Church, and supporters of the King of Spain opposed Morelos's program; most people were for it.

However, not much time was given to Morelos and the other leaders to make the Constitution work. Independence still had to be won on the battlefield, and the Insurgents were finding it harder to win victories. General Calleja, now Viceroy, was attacking with greater determination, and his forces were growing larger. The leaders of the Congress were quarreling with each other. Some were jealous, others were eager for power. Morelos was not always able to act on his own, as he often had to wait until the Congress made up its mind.

Morelos attacked Valladolid, where he was beaten back by Viceroy Calleja and General Iturbide. Against the advice of his generals, Morelos cut short his retreat and turned about to face the Royalists in battle again. He was beaten once more. One of his ablest generals, Mariano Matamoros, a former priest, was captured and put to death. When Morelos heard the news, he exclaimed, "I have lost my left arm."

From that point on, the situation grew worse for Morelos and his men. The Congress took away his supreme command and appointed leaders who were unfit. Each tried to get something for himself from the district he ruled. Then Morelos received another hard blow. Another of his able generals, his friend Hermenegildo

Galeana, whom he called his right arm, was killed in battle. "Now I have lost both my arms," Morelos cried out. "Now I am nothing! "

In September 1815, after many defeats and desertions, the cause of the Insurgents seemed hopeless. The government and Congress tried to escape to Tehuacán, which is on the road to Veracruz. They thought they would be in a better position to reach the coast and get help from the United States. Morelos and a small band of armed men went to protect them.

Calleja learned about the attempted escape, and sent soldiers to find them. Morelos had cleverly covered up his movements, but by accident one of the Royalist parties came upon Morelos and his men. The Insurgents were frightened, but Morelos rallied them and prepared to fight. His men were beaten by the larger number of the Royalists.

Morelos saw that all was lost, but wanting to save the government and the Congress, he sent them one way while he went toward a steep hill to attract the Royalists. He was captured by Royalists led by a deserter, Lieutenant Matías Carranco. Morelos coolly said to him as he surrendered, "Señor Carranco, it seems that we know each other, for we have met before."

Morelos was taken to Mexico City, and a few hours after arrival there on November 22, 1815, his trial began. He was tried by the military, the state, the Church, and the Inquisition. Although he defended himself bravely, he was found guilty, and was executed by a firing squad on December 22, 1815 in a little village near Mexico City. Disturbances were feared if he were put to death in the city.

At first he was buried in the village, but later his body was moved to the Mexico City Cathedral, and then to the crypt, or underground room, below the Monument of Independence, where other heroes of the War of Independence, including Father Hidalgo, Mariano Matamoros, and Nicolás Bravo are also buried.

Morelos has been honored as have few other heroes in Mexican history. In Morelia, the house that he bought in 1810, Casa de Morelos, is now a museum and a national shrine which contains many objects that once belonged to him. Many Mexican coins and stamps bear the likeness of Morelos. He appears in many mural paintings, especially in those by Diego Rivera in Cuernavaca, and by José Clemente Orozco in the Governor's Palace in Guadalajara. Monuments in his honor are found all over Mexico.

The best known of these monuments is the huge statue that

Statue of José María Morelos at fishing village,
Lake Pátzcuaro

rises above Lake Pátzcuaro a few miles south of Morelia, the work
of the sculptor Guillermo Ruiz. The statue was put up by order of
Governor Lázaro Cárdenas of Michoacán, later President of
Mexico, a great admirer of Morelos. From the shore of the lake,
this statue can be seen on top of an island called Janitzio. The
right hand is held upright to the sky. Cárdenas meant this statue
on the island to be like the Statue of Liberty on an island in New
York harbor.

The people of Mexico have honored and remembered Morelos
for the work he did to advance the cause of liberty and social
progress. In 1823, only two years after they had won their
independence, they honored him with the title *Benemérito de la
Patria*, "Well-Deserving of the Country."

71

10

LEONA VICARIO

HEROINE OF THE INSURGENTS

While Morelos was fighting against the Spaniards, help came from unexpected places. One of the most unusual supporters of the Insurgents was a young lady, Señorita Leona Vicario. Her action was extraordinary because women did not take part in public life at that time. Besides, she was rich, and Morelos was fighting for the poor.

Leona Vicario was born of Creole parents in Mexico City on April 10, 1789. Her father was a lawyer, her mother was well-educated. Leona received a good education, having studied fine arts, science, literature, history, and singing. She also loved to paint and was a good speaker. She was fond of serious reading, especially of books on politics, not only in Spanish but also in French and German.

She grew up to be a strong girl of normal height, full of energy. Her eyes were bright black, and she had a pleasant, gracious look. Although kind and friendly, she could be firm.

Leona's world began to change when she reached eighteen. Her father and mother both died in 1807, and her uncle, Agustín Pomposo Fernando de San Salvador, became her guardian. He was an important person in Mexico City, a lawyer with some connections with the law school and university. An arrangement was made by which Leona lived in a house next to her uncle's.

A young man of about her own age named Andrés Quintana Roo, better known as Quintana Roo, now came into her life. He arrived in Mexico City in 1808. He was handsome and dressed in expensive, elegant clothes. At the time, he was a poet and made a wonderful impression on Leona.

Quintana Roo had come from Mérida, capital of Yucatán, to study, first at the university, and then at the law school in Mexico City. Don Agustín had met him, handed him his diploma at the university, and taken him into his house, where he helped with legal affairs.

Leona and Quintana fell in love and wanted to get married. They needed permission of Don Agustín, who refused to give it. Meanwhile, the War of Independence broke out. Both Quintana Roo and Leona Vicario favored the Insurgents. Roo left Mexico City to join the Insurgents and soon became one of their leaders.

Leona, of course, stayed at home, but managed to get letters through to Roo, and even sent supplies. She also got men to join the Insurgents. Such actions were very bold and courageous, but also very dangerous. Her uncle was a Royalist; she was living in the capital city of the Viceroy and Spanish power. However, she was willing to risk her life for the freedom of Mexico.

Her activities were soon discovered. Some of her letters were seized and taken to the authorities. In May, 1813, she was arrested and placed in a convent as a prisoner. One day, three men on horseback drove up. Two of them blocked the doors, the third ran to her room and carried her down. She was rescued, and an extra horse had been taken along for her!

She managed to reach a small village near Mexico City, where she hid. Some of her friends and relations found out where she was staying and tried to get her to return home. Leona realized that soon the authorities might also find her. She left and went to the camp of the Insurgents, where she found Quintana Roo and married him.

The government of the Viceroy declared her a traitor and took away her property. After the execution of Morelos, amnesty, or pardon, was offered to all who had fought against the government. Quintana Roo and Leona took advantage of this, but her property

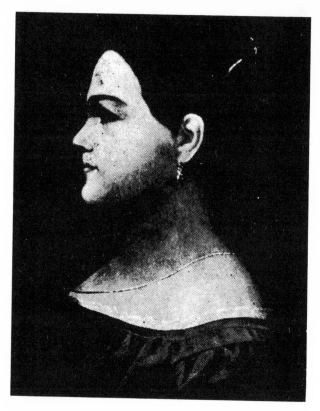

Leona Vicario

was not returned. They were now very poor.

In 1822, after independence had been won, the Mexican Congress gave her an hacienda in the state of Hidalgo and a sum of money. Quintana Roo became active in public life again and was elected to Congress. He spoke up against the harsh policies of President Anastasio Bustamente. Leona also showed her courage by telling Bustamente that he was not a sultan but a president of a free republic.

Quintana Roo devoted himself to education and became the honorary head of a new academy, at the same time returning to writing poetry. Leona took care of the hacienda and brought up their two daughters. She died on August 21, 1842.

The territory of Quintana Roo next to his native Yucatán was named after him. A national primary school was named after her, and her picture appeared on a stamp some years ago. They are honored today as a hero and a heroine of Mexican Independence.

11

FRANCISCO JAVIER MINA

A SPANIARD HONORED BY MEXICO

After the death of Morelos, help came to the Insurgents from another unexpected place.

The Mexicans who fought to free their country from Spanish rule hated the Spaniards . One Spaniard, however, came to help them, and they hold him in great honor today!

He is Francisco Javier (Xavier) Mina, who was born in July, 1789 in Otano, Navarre. He studied at Pampeluna (Pamplona) in Navarre, and in 1807, had just entered the University of Saragossa (Zaragoza).

He gave up his studies because there was a fever for fighting among the Spaniards. It was the period of the Napoleonic Wars, when Napoleon invaded Spain. There was also great unrest because many Spaniards wanted the constitution of their country changed to give the people more freedom.

Francisco met a retired colonel who gave him ideas of fighting for reforms. Francisco's uncle, Francisco Espoz Mina, only eight years older than young Francisco, was going off to fight, and later won a great reputation as a guerrilla fighter against Napoleon's army. He also opposed King Ferdinand VII of Spain.

The younger Mina joined his uncle and also became a great guerrilla fighter. However, he was captured by the French after a year of fighting and was sent to a prison in Vincennes, near Paris, where he remained for about five years. When he returned to Spain in about 1815, King Ferdinand was not happy to have him there because of his liberal ideas. Since Francisco's uncle had been exiled for the same reason, the younger Mina decided to get out of Spain.

He went to England, then the most liberal country in Europe. There he met many Mexicans who had run away from their homeland. He learned from them about the fight for freedom and the deaths of Hidalgo and Morelos. This made him decide that his place was in Mexico as a fighter for freedom!

Wealthy Englishmen like Lord Holland, who sympathized with the Mexicans, encouraged and helped Mina. They gave him money for a ship, and in May 1816, he sailed from Liverpool with about twenty English, French, Italian and Spanish officers on board. He went to a number of cities in the United States, such as Norfolk, Virginia, New York, Philadelphia, and Baltimore, to raise money and enlist men. Mr. Dennis Smith of Baltimore, who was most sympathetic, helped him greatly, and Mina recruited about 300 American, British, French, Irish, and Italian volunteers. Some were adventurers, others were anxious to help the people fighting for liberty.

Early in 1817, Mina had a fleet of seven ships, with which he set sail for Mexico. On the way he stopped in Haiti, New Orleans, and Galveston, Texas. About April 15, his troops landed at Soto la Marina, a small port on the northeastern coast of Mexico.

In the short time that he was in Mexico, Mina made many speeches and declarations that show the noble ideas that prompted him to go there. To his soldiers he said: "We have come to New Spain not to conquer but to emancipate! " To the Spaniards whom he urged to join him, he declared:

"Let history show that if there were Spaniards who conquered this land with cruelty and greed, there were also Spaniards who offered their blood and their lives for the freedom of the Mexicans! "

Mina built a fort at Soto la Marina, left a hundred men to guard it, and marched inland. He won a number of victories against much larger Royalist armies. Viceroy Juan Ruiz de Apodaca offered him a high position in the Royalist army if he would come over to

Francisco Javier Mina

his side, but Mina refused. While he was marching south, the Viceroy sent an army against the fort, which had to surrender. Mina kept on winning victories and joined forces with a daring Insurgent leader, Pedro Moreno, who held a strong place called Sombrero Fort in the neighborhood of Guanajuato.

The Viceroy, who thought that the Revolution was over when Morelos was executed and so many thousands of the Insurgents had accepted his offer of amnesty or gone into hiding, now saw the struggle rising up strongly again. He therefore sent a large army with orders to wipe out Mina and his army.

Part of the Royalist army attacked the Sombrero Fort. Mina and Moreno were unable to hold it, because the supply of water and food was giving out. They had to escape from the fort. The Royalists killed all the prisoners, including the sick and wounded.

On August 26, 1817, Mina and Moreno met again at Silao, not far from Guanajuato. They had only sixty men with them. Suddenly the Royalists fell upon them, killing Moreno and taking Mina prisoner. He was shot as a traitor on November 11, 1817. However, his campaign had helped the Insurgents; Mina gave them new courage and time to rally their forces!

Pedro Moreno

He was only twenty-eight years old and had spent most of his active life fighting against oppression—against Napoleon, Ferdinand VII, and the Spaniards in Mexico.

Mina had been in Mexico for only a few months, having come, not in search of adventure, conquest, or wealth for himself, but freedom for the Mexicans. That is why they have kept his name alive by giving it to streets and towns and districts throughout Mexico. That is also why they honored this man in 1823 with the title *Benemérito de la Patria en Grado Heroico*, "Well-Deserving of the Country with the Rank of Hero."

Later, the Mexicans honored him again. His body was moved to its resting place beneath the Monument of Independence in Mexico City; his statue is at the base. He is the only Spaniard who has been so honored. The eternal flame of that Monument burns as brightly for him, a Spaniard, as it does for the other heroes of the War of Independence, Mexicans who fought against the Spaniards and who rest there with him!

12

VICENTE GUERRERO

A FIGHTER TO THE END

The Spanish word *guerrero* means a warrior, a fighter. Vicente Guerrero, a great Mexican patriot, lived up to the meaning of his name. He fought almost all the years of his life, first for the independence of his country, and then against corrupt or treacherous Mexicans.

He was born in August 1782 (or 1783) in Tixtla, in the southern part of Mexico. Guerrero was the son of a peon, a very poor farm worker. He himself became a muleteer. He was thin but strong, had a large nose, a very dark complexion, and thick lips. It is thought that one of his ancestors was a Negro.

Guerrero hated the Spaniards and soon gathered other poor workers and Indians to fight against them. They were called the Guadalupe Regiment, and Guerrero was their captain. Soon they joined the forces of Morelos and helped him capture Tixtla.

After the death of Morelos in December 1815, a few leaders continued the fight for independence in different parts of the country. Near Veracruz they were led by Félix Fernández, who changed his name to Guadalupe Victoria. In the south, Guerrero carried on guerrilla warfare with about 1,000 tough fighters from the mountain regions. Only Victoria and Guerrero, of all the important leaders, refused to accept the pardon offered by the Viceroy.

Guerrero carried on the war from the mountains near Acapulco. The Royalist soldiers kept coming after him and his men. Many of his followers became discouraged and left him. Food and water were becoming scarce. Still, Guerrero never lost hope. At one time, he was the only important leader still carrying on the fight.

Then a most unexpected turnabout occurred. General Agustín de Iturbide was sent by the Viceroy to destroy the army of Guerrero and bring the revolution to an end. Iturbide had convinced the Viceroy that with an army of 2,500 men he could wipe out the Insurgents.

Vicente Guerrero

Instead, he himself was ambushed by a leader named Pedro Ascencio de Alquisirias who had joined Guerrero, and he was forced to retreat. Guerrero himself had defeated and wiped out a whole company of crack Royalist soldiers in another battle.

Iturbide was now in deep trouble as he had been accused of stealing public funds and had wasted his own fortune. He would be absolutely disgraced if he went back to Mexico City a defeated man. Therefore he proposed to Guerrero that they should join forces and fight against the Viceroy to free Mexico from the Spaniards.

At first Guerrero did not trust Iturbide. Finally, he consented because he saw a chance of bringing freedom and peace to Mexico at last. Iturbide, on the other hand, was ambitious and selfish. He would take any action to get what he wanted for himself, in this case, power.

The two men met. A plan was drawn up known as the Plan of Iguala from the name of the place where it was written out. Another name for it is *Las Tres Garantías*, the Three Guarantees, which are (1) Mexico would be an independent constitutional monarchy (2) All the people would be citizens, without castes, or classes, with no differences among Spanish, Creoles, mestizos, and Indians (3) The Catholic religion would be the official religion of Mexico.

Guerrero had a hard decision to make. There was nothing in the Plan of Iguala about dividing up the large farms, giving land to the Indians, and improving conditions for the poor. Still, he accepted the Plan. The war had gone on for eleven years. A few leaders and small bands might keep the Viceroy's armies busy, but without more support, victory seemed far away. Guerrero may have hoped that once independence was won, reforms would follow.

People all over Mexico supported the Plan of Iguala. Military leaders who were in hiding now joined Guerrero and Iturbide. Town after town deserted from the Viceroy; officials in the government went over to Iturbide.

A new Viceroy, Don Juan O'Donojú, arrived on July 30, 1821. He met Iturbide and signed a treaty at Córdoba accepting the Plan of Iguala for Spain. On September 27, 1821, Iturbide, Guerrero, and Guadalupe Victoria marched into Mexico City at the head of "The Army of the Three Guarantees." At last Mexico was free from Spanish rule.

A new government had to be formed. According to the Plan of

General Agustín de Iturbide

Iguala, a council, or junta, chose men to elect a congress, which then would draw up a new constitution. Ferdinand VII refused to have anything to do with the Plan of Iguala or the Treaty of Córdoba.

While the congress was debating without getting anywhere, some soldiers shouted, "Long live Agustín I, Emperor of Mexico! " The crowds joined in demanding that Iturbide be their emperor. On July 22, 1822, Iturbide became Emperor Agustín I of Mexico. He proved to be an unpopular ruler. General Antonio López de Santa Anna, Guerrero, and other men who were not happy at the way the agreement with Iturbide had turned out, revolted.

Base of the Independence Monument

Guerrero, Nicolás Bravo, a hero of the fight for independence, and Anastasio Bustamente, a former Royalist officer, left Mexico City to fight against Iturbide. They were beaten, and Guerrero was badly wounded. Santa Anna was ready to give up the fight and run away to another country when Iturbide's army revolted near Veracruz and joined Santa Anna. Iturbide then gave up the throne on March 19, 1823.

Congress appointed three men to govern Mexico until a legal government could be set up. Nicolás Bravo and Guerrero were two of these men. On October 10, 1824, Guadalupe Victoria became the first constitutional president of Mexico. His rival was Nicolás Bravo. Disappointed at not being elected President, Bravo revolted against President Victoria. Guerrero put down the revolt. Since Victoria was a kind person, he did not have Bravo put to death for treason but sent him into exile.

At the next election in 1828, Manuel Gómez Pedraza became President with the help of the rich and the army. Guerrero, his opponent, complained that he had been cheated and rose up against Pedraza. Santa Anna and other leading men joined Guerrero. Pedraza resigned, and Guerrero became President on April 1, 1829, with Bustamente as Vice-President.

Guerrero found it easier to fight enemies on the field of battle than in the government. His enemies accused him of having become President by violence. They ridiculed him for his lack of education. People who could not get jobs in the government blamed him. The government was poor and unable to pay the salaries of its workers.

Vice-President Bustamente, who had sworn to be loyal to Guerrero, revolted. Guerrero left Mexico City to put down the rebellion. As soon as he left, the soldiers in the capital went over to the side of the rebels. Nicolás Bravo, who had come back from exile, also led a rebellion against Guerrero, who retreated to the south of Mexico, a part of the country with which he was very familiar.

There he received help from Juan Álvarez, a very powerful ranch owner. Many of Guerrero's former followers came to fight at his side. They held back the troops of Bustamente for a year. Finally, treachery won for the government what it could not win on the battlefield. Antonio Facio, Minister of War, offered the captain of an Italian ship, Antonio Picaluga, a large sum of money if he could get Guerrero into the Government's hands. Guerrero and the Captain had met in Mexico City and were on friendly terms. Picaluga agreed.

On January 14, 1830, he invited Guerrero, who was in Acapulco, to come aboard his ship for a banquet. Guerrero, a very trusting person, did not suspect any tricks from a person he considered to be his friend. On board the ship, the captain had a few of his crew act as if they were going to mutiny. He told Guerrero to go into the captain's cabin for safety. Then he locked the door and set sail.

When they reached the next port, Picaluga handed Guerrero over to the government officials. Guerrero was taken to Oaxaca, put on trial for treason, found guilty, and was executed on February 14, 1831 at Cuilapa, for which he has been called "The Martyr of Cuilapa." The nation was shocked. Picaluga was condemned to death in Italy for his treacherous action, but he never went back to face the penalty.

The Mexican people have honored Guerrero as a brave fighter in the War for Independence. A state was named after him. His name is written in golden letters, together with the names of other heroes, in one of the government buildings in Mexico City. He has been honored with the title *Benemérito de la Patria*, "Well-Deserving of the Country." His statue is at the base of the Monument of Independence in Mexico City together with the statues of Hidalgo, Morelos, Bravo, and Mina.

13

BENITO JUÁREZ

THE ABRAHAM LINCOLN OF MEXICO

Benito Juárez has been called the Abraham Lincoln of Mexico. They both lived at about the same time. Juárez was born on March 21, 1806, Lincoln was born in 1809. Lincoln died in 1865, Juárez in 1872. Both came from very poor families. As boys, both were fond of books and learning, and taught themselves. They both went in for law and politics. Juárez and Lincoln became the Presidents of their countries, and fought for the rights of the oppressed. Both of them were engaged in civil wars.

Benito Juárez (full name Benito Pablo Juárez y García) was born in the tiny mountain village of San Pablo Guelatao in the state of Oaxaca. His parents were Zapotec Indians.

When Juárez was about fifty years old, he wrote the story of his life for his children. He says that he never knew his parents, who died when he was three years old. At first, Benito and two of his three sisters were taken care of by his father's parents, who died a few years later. The boy was then sent to his uncle, Bernardino Juárez, a poor man who supported himself by hard work. Still, he looked after his nephew as well as he could.

There was no school in the village. The uncle tried to teach Benito Spanish. He also thought that the only career open to a poor boy like Benito was in the Church as a priest. Young Benito was very excited about learning Spanish. He would carry a whip to his uncle with which to beat him if he did not learn his lesson well!

The uncle and the boy tried hard, but they had little free time. Benito worked in the fields looking after sheep, but he did not give up trying to get an education. The children of a family with money could go to school in Oaxaca, a large city. A poor boy, like Benito, might work as a servant of a rich family in the city, and in return would be taught to read and write. On December 17, 1818, when he was only twelve years old, he left the house and walked all the way to Oaxaca, forty-one miles away, over mountain roads more than 5,000 feet high.

In Oaxaca, young Juárez went to a house where his sister was working as a cook. He stayed there a few weeks, earning his keep by helping out, meanwhile looking for work. He found a very good man, Don Antonio Salanueva, a bookbinder, who was eager to help boys who wanted to learn. He took Benito into his home and taught him reading and writing.

Benito worked in Don Antonio's house doing many jobs. He washed floors, ran errands, took care of plants, and washed dishes. In between his daily tasks he studied and read. There was great love and affection between Don Antonio and the little Indian boy who felt so keenly the need of somebody to take the place of a father.

Juárez soon began to go to a primary school. He entered the fourth grade. Only reading and writing, but no Spanish grammar, were taught there. The boy did not like the method, which was mainly learning by heart and repeating what had been learned. He changed to another school, where the teacher gave him a paper to follow as a model. Juárez admits that his work was not perfect. However, the teacher did not correct his mistakes or teach him how to do better. Instead, he punished him.

Angered at this injustice, Benito left the school. There were no other elementary schools to go to, and he began to teach himself once more. He used to see students coming from a seminary, a school where they were learning to become priests. This made him remember how his uncle had wanted him to become a priest. Although he really did not want to become one, he realized that these students were supposed to know very much and were honored by the people.

He asked Don Antonio to let him go to the seminary, and promised to repay him by working in the house. Don Antonio, now his godfather, encouraged him. Juárez took the necessary courses. He studied Latin grammar, the arts, philosophy, and theology, and received excellent grades.

However, a change took place in Mexico that made it possible for him to go to a different kind of school. After Mexico had won its independence, new types of colleges were opened which were not run by the Church. Even the sons of the poor could study to be doctors or lawyers instead of priests. In 1828, at age 22, Juárez entered one of these new colleges, the Institute of Arts and Sciences at Oaxaca, supporting himself by doing odd jobs. After Juárez finished his law courses in 1831, he first served as an alderman and then as a member of the State Legislature. He passed the bar examinations in 1834, practiced law, and twice served as a judge.

On July 31, 1843, he married Margarita Maza, the daughter of the persons with whom he had first stayed on his arrival in Oaxaca in 1818. She was seventeen, he was thirty-seven. They had twelve children, three boys and nine girls.

In 1847, Juárez was elected Governor of the state of Oaxaca. He was a member of the Liberal Party, which stood for improving the conditions of the poor. He was one of the best governors in Mexican history. Because he remembered how hard it had been for a poor boy like himself to go to school, he saw to it that many schools were built, and Indians were trained to become teachers. More girls went to school while he was governor than ever before in Mexico. By strict honesty and the careful spending of money and collecting of taxes, he managed to lower the state's debt.

President Santa Anna was an enemy of the Liberals and especially of Juárez. After Juárez's term of office ended in 1852, Santa Anna gave him no peace. He sent orders forcing him to go from one place to another. Finally, Juárez was arrested and without a trial, he was put in prison in Veracruz. The charge was that he had not gone where he had been ordered. His wife went into hiding.

Juárez was then placed on a British ship bound for England. He was able to get off at Havana, and sailed to New Orleans, arriving there on December 29, 1853. He met a number of Mexicans living in exile with whom he formed plans to overthrow Santa Anna.

Juárez left New Orleans on June 20, 1855. When he arrived in Mexico he learned that Santa Anna had been driven from power. There was no legal government. Three different groups, the Liberal Party, which wanted reforms, the Conservative Party, which wanted no changes, and the Monarchists, which wanted a ruler like an emperor, were all struggling for power.

General Juan Álvarez, a mestizo with Negro blood, who had led the revolt against Santa Anna and had once helped Guerrero, became the President of Mexico. He made Juárez his Minister of Justice. Juárez immediately had a law passed that took away the right of the Church and army to have their own courts.

In 1856, General Álvarez was replaced by General Ignacio Comonfort, a Liberal who had also fought against Santa Anna. In 1857, Juárez became his Vice-President, President of the Supreme Court, and next in line for the office of President. A new constitution was set up which took away a great part of the Church's power.

The Church and the Conservatives were against the new constitution. The opposition leader was General Félix Zuloaga. who demanded that Comonfort get rid of it. Zuloaga and a group of armed men broke into the National Palace, drove out the Congress, and locked up Juárez, who wanted the constitution kept. Comonfort was forced to put an end to the new constitution. He escaped and fled to New York, but he set Juárez free before he left.

The Conservatives declared that Zuloaga was now President of Mexico; actually, he began his rule as a military dictator. Mexico really had two presidents, because when Comonfort was not able to complete his term of office, Juárez, as President of the Supreme Court and Vice President, legally became the President. Moreover, Liberals and liberal governors meeting at Querétaro, supported Juárez as the President.

Juárez slipped out of Mexico City on January 12, 1858 with a few companions and reached Guanajuato. On the 19th he declared that the legal government of Mexico had been set up there. He formed a cabinet and issued proclamations. A civil war was now

Benito Pablo Juárez

on between the Liberals and Conservatives. Supporters of the Catholic Church headed by General Tomás Mejía, an Indian, and General Miguel Miramón of French descent, helped the Conservatives.

The cause of the people depended on a little man, an Indian only about five feet in height. His shortness was emphasized by his small hands and feet. However, he was strong and healthy. His dark face was clean-shaven, with deep-set eyes that seemed to be staring at a person. His black hair was parted on the left side. He usually wore a dark suit, a white shirt, a large bow tie, and a watch chain over his vest.

In the civil war one of his generals was defeated by Zuloaga's army, and Juárez and his government fled to Guadalajara. His men mutineed, partly because he had no money with which to pay them. The mutineers were about to shoot him. He heard the command, "Aim! " and waited for the final shot. One of his followers rushed in front of him and cried out. "Put up your weapons. Brave men are not murderers." The soldiers did not shoot, and set him and his followers free.

Juárez had to leave Guadalajara. His armies had suffered defeats, and his chief general had surrendered with all his men. Juárez had only 350 men left to fight on his side. He decided to go to Veracruz, which was held by Liberal, or Constitutionalist, forces.

Veracruz is a long distance from Guadalajara. Juárez and his companions could not make their way over the mountains against the hostile armies. They first went to Manzanillo on the Pacific coast, where they waited for a ship to come along. On April 11, they boarded an American steamer bound for Panama. There they went overland to the Caribbean Sea. (This was before the Panama Canal was built.) Then they took a steamer at Colón and reached New Orleans by way of Havana. On May 1, they sailed from New Orleans, reaching Veracruz on the 4th of May, 1858.

Here Juárez was joined by his wife, Doña Margarita. The story of her march over the mountain trails from Oaxaca to Veracruz is a heroic tale. She had to take along eight of their children, the oldest, fourteen years old, the youngest, a baby. Making her way over the difficult trails for about 300 miles, she took a month for the trip.

The military government was now headed by General Miramón, who attacked Veracruz but was beaten off. Guerrilla warfare was taking place all over Mexico. Many supporters of Juárez were urging him to give up the Constitution, thinking they could win over Mirámon and his followers and bring peace. Juárez showed an iron will. He would not have all the years of fighting for the betterment of the people wasted.

In a short time the war began to go against Miramón. Many of his men deserted. He lost two battles to the Liberals, and his government fell; he fled to France.

Juárez returned to Mexico City on January 11, 1861 as the legal President of Mexico. Like Lincoln, Juárez was faced with the problem of putting the pieces together again after a bloody war. He still had many enemies. There were those who hated him because of his actions against the Church. Many bands of guerrillas called reactionaries were still fighting, especially under the leadership of General Leonardo Márquez, known as the Tiger of Tacubaya for his cruelty.

The government was almost bankrupt. The cost of keeping up an army was great. Mexico was in debt to foreign countries, especially England, France, Spain, and the United States, and had to delay paying its debts. Opponents of Juárez blamed him for all of Mexico's troubles and wanted him to resign.

The governments of England, France, and Spain decided to send troops to collect the money owed to them. They invited the United States also, but that country was involved in its own civil war and refused. However, the other countries went ahead in spite of the Monroe Doctrine, which declares that foreign nations are not to interfere in the affairs of countries in North and South America.

In December, 1861, an army of 6,000 Spanish soldiers landed in Veracruz. A month later, 700 British marines and 2,500 French soldiers followed. After talks among the Mexicans and representatives of the foreign countries, the Spaniards and British agreed to go home. The French stayed in Mexico and took up their position in Orizaba, between Mexico City and Veracruz. More troops were sent by Napoleon III.

Part of the French army, about 6,000 men, began to march to Mexico City. On the way they first had to take the fortified city of Puebla commanded by Ignacio Zaragoza, an experienced guerrilla fighter. On May 5, 1862, he beat off the French charge, attacked them, and drove them back to the coast. This was the first defeat of a French army in many years. May 5 is a Mexican national holiday.

Napoleon III was angered at what a ragged army of a poor country had done to his crack fighting men. He sent about 30,000 more troops. In Mexico they were joined by Conservative Mexicans. Among their leaders were Generals Márquez, Mejía, and Miramón, who had returned from France. The French attacked Puebla again and forced it to surrender on May 16, 1863. The road to Mexico City was now open.

On May 31, Juárez and a few members of his government left Mexico City for San Luis Potosí. The French forces were too large to be resisted by the small number of defenders in the capital. Once again Juárez became an exile and a wanderer, driven out by enemies. But, he had courage and perseverance; he did not give up.

He formed a new cabinet and gathered a new army. Comonfort, the former President, now dedicated to Constitutional government, became commander-in-chief. Juárez received a great blow when Comonfort was ambushed and killed. The troubles of Juárez and his government increased. They moved from place to place, ending up in Monterrey in the north. Some of his generals deserted, others became traitors. Some help came from the Americans when a small number of volunteers crossed into Mexico to fight on his side.

Still, the French and their Mexican supporters pushed on and drove Juárez out of Monterrey. Juárez himself was almost killed when his carriage was shot through with bullets. Juárez and a few friends went into hiding in the desert regions of northern Mexico.

For some years a number of Mexicans living in Europe, enemies of the Constitutionalist government, had been scheming to turn Mexico into a monarchy. They wanted to put a European prince on the throne. Their choice was the Archduke Maximilian of Austria, brother of the Emperor of the Austro-Hungarian Empire. He was then a young man of about thirty. Napoleon III promised to help Maximilian, who was ambitious, and when a group of Mexicans asked him to come over, he accepted. He landed in Veracruz on May 28, 1864.

Maximilian was accompanied by his wife, the beautiful Carlota, who was thrilled with the idea of becoming an Empress. A small Mexican army opposing the French was led by a young general named Porfirio Díaz. He had to fight against an army of a few thousand Mexican traitors and 35,000 French soldiers led by General Achille François Bazaine. Díaz was defeated at Oaxaca and surrendered. He soon made a remarkable and daring escape and began to fight again from the state of Guerrero.

In spite of military victories Maximilian faced trouble. His treasury was low because of the great cost of palace life and of the army. The Civil War in the United States had ended, and President Andrew Johnson, who had succeeded Abraham Lincoln, might call upon the Monroe Doctrine and ask that foreign troops get out of Mexico.

Maximilian could no longer expect help from his friends in Europe. The Austrians had been attacked and defeated by the Germans. Napoleon III, fearing the Germans, and realizing that the American government would soon ask him to withdraw the French troops, sent word to General Bazaine to begin sending the French army home.

General Bazaine advised Maximilian to go back to Europe. He was willing, but Carlota, still wanting to remain an Empress, persuaded him to stay. She went to Europe to see Napoleon III and even the Pope to get help. When they refused to assist her, she went out of her mind. She lived on, an insane woman, until 1927.

She never saw her husband again.

In Mexico the situation was becoming worse for Maximilian, who had become unpopular with most Mexicans. The armies of Juárez (also called "Republicans," and "of the Republic") were growing larger, and were recapturing cities once held by the French. Maximilian was unable to decide whether to leave Mexico or stay. The Mexican generals on his side, who would be ruined if he left, urged him to stay. As the forces of the Republic closed in, he left Mexico City with an army of 1,500 men and reached Querétaro, a city friendly to him. There he found five of his generals, all Mexicans, and an army of 7,500 men.

Meanwhile, Juárez was in San Luis Potosí, directing the Republican Government and making decisions, while his generals, at the head of an army of 27,000, surrounded Querétaro. Maximilian's army began to suffer from a scarcity of food and water. The Republican generals sent him an offer of freedom if he surrendered his army to them, but he refused. Then one of his own officers, Colonel Miguel López, let the forces of Juárez enter the city. (Even the Mexicans would have nothing to do with López later for this act of treachery.) Maximilian and his officers surrendered at a place near the city, Cerro de las Campanas, Hill of the Bells.

Attempts were made to rescue Maximilian, but he turned them down. He refused to escape while those who fought at his side suffered. Prominent persons in the United States and Europe appealed to Juárez to spare Maximilian, but he said that whatever happened to him was the will of the people. Maximilian was tried together with Generals Mejía and Miramón. The charges were that he had ordered Mexican prisoners to be put to death, and that all had conspired against the independence of Mexico. By a vote of four to three, a court-martial condemned all three to death. On June 19, 1867, Maximilian, Mejía, and Miramón were shot by a firing squad on the Hill of the Bells. Maximilian died calmly and nobly.

While these events were going on, General Porfirio Díaz was meeting with great success elsewhere. He captured Mexico City, allowed the French and Austrian troops to leave for Veracruz on their way to Europe, and forced the Mexican troops to surrender. He then prepared the capital for the return of President Juárez. Leaving San Luis Potosí on July 3, 1867, Juárez arrived in Mexico City on July 15. His wife and six of his children, five unmarried daughters and his only living son, returned to Mexico City about ten days later. They had been in New Orleans for safety, and had been helped by the United States government to sail home.

At last Mexico seemed to be at peace, but there was no peace for Benito Juárez. The problems of Mexico were still too great to be solved in a short time or even in a longer time by any one man. The country was poor, and there was little trade or industry. There were many traitors who had fought against the government and were still unfriendly to it. There were others who had fought for it, but only because they thought they had something to gain. When the war was over, they tried to get power. There were many men who had been soldiers all their lives, and they found it hard to settle down. They roamed over the countryside as bandits. There was little trade with other countries, because they did not trust the Mexicans, and the Mexicans, in turn, were suspicious of them because they interfered in Mexican affairs.

Juárez was elected President again in 1867. He discharged most of the troops but kept enough of them to put down any guerrilla warfare. He had British engineers complete a railway from Veracruz to Mexico City and devised a school system that was modern for his time. In spite of Mexico's troubles, he was popular with most of the people, but not with Porfirio Díaz, who had lost his army and gone back to the state of Oaxaca to raise sugar cane.

In addition to the cares of running the country, Juárez had personal troubles. He suffered a stroke in October, 1870. On January 2, 1871, his devoted wife, Margarita, died at age 44 after a long illness. She was an unselfish woman who had gone through many hardships and had moved about not only from city to city but even out of the country as her husband's political fortunes changed. In addition, she had seen five of their twelve children die.

She was mourned by thousands as the funeral procession made its way through the streets of Mexico City. Juárez was so stunned that he found it impossible to work for at least a month. Señora de Juárez was a remarkable woman, and in her quiet way, a heroine of Mexico.

Feeling that his great task was still unfinished, Juárez decided to run for President again in 1871. In this election, he was opposed by two other candidates, Porfirio Díaz and Sebastian Lerdo de Tejeda. The result was close, but Juárez won the run-off in Congress by a large margin, and took office on December 1, 1871.

Juárez's last days were filled with more sadness. Rebellions broke out. One of them was led by Félix Díaz, brother of Porfirio.

He and others planned to place Porfirio in power as temporary President in place of Juárez. The rebellion was put down. Porfirio escaped and went into hiding, but Félix was caught and shot to death.

On July 18, 1872, Benito Juárez complained of severe pains near the heart. He was told by his doctor that he had a heart attack and that there was no hope of recovery. Juárez received the news with the courage and calmness that he had showed all his life. He died just before midnight, at 66 years of age.

Juárez was a quiet and reserved person, whose pictures never show him with a smile. Even those who liked him found him mysterious, but they respected him. He devoted his life to one great aim: improving the life of the people of Mexico. Unlike many others who came to power, he was thoroughly honest and led a simple life.

He is looked upon as the greatest of all Mexicans, as one who did more for the people than any other Mexican leader. Some of his reforms became a lasting part of the Mexican Constitution. His effort to bring education to all is still one of Mexico's major programs.

Juárez has been honored in many ways. The city of El Paso del Norte, one of the many places in which he set up a temporary residence, has been renamed Ciudad Juárez, or Juárez City. It is the largest Mexican city on the Rio Grande at the border with the United States. In the National Palace in Mexico City, there is a bronze statue of Benito Juárez. Near it is the entrance to the *Recinto de Juárez* "Juárez Corner," which contains the rooms in which Juárez lived and his library. Also in Mexico City, there is a large white marble monument in the shape of a semi-circle. It is called the Benito Juárez Hemicycle (Half-Circle), and was erected in his honor in 1910.

There are many Mexican stamps with the picture of Juárez. Orozco painted remarkable murals of Juárez and his times in the Museum of History at Chapultepec, once the palace of Maximilian and Carlota. March 21, Juárez's birthday, is a Mexican national holiday.

Juárez has been called the Great Emancipator. Like George Washington, he did not lose courage in the darkest days of the fighting, and for this reason he is known as *El Impasible*, "The Imperturbable," one who is unmoved by misfortune. His name is often coupled with the title *El Hombre Ejemplar*, "The Exemplary

Man," a person who is worthy of imitation because of his good qualities. As a hero not merely of Mexico but of humanity, he has earned the title *Benemérito de las Américas,* "Well-Deserving of the Americas."

One of his greatest memorials, which is so fitting to our times and by which he will long be remembered, is found in his own words:

"Let the people and government respect the rights of all—among individuals as among nations peace is respect for the rights of others."

Benito Pablo Juárez

14

PANCHO VILLA

BANDIT OR HERO?

There is a small museum in the little town of Hidalgo del Parral in the state of Chihuahua in northern Mexico. This museum keeps alive the memory of Pancho Villa, who was shot to death in this town. It contains even the automobile which he was driving when bullets ended his life. As late as April 1969, his widow, Señora Luz de Villa, was in charge of this museum. She was 75 years old and had devoted more than forty years to clear her husband's reputation.

There are different opinions about Pancho Villa. To some persons he was a murderer and a bandit. To others he was a fool who had impossible dreams. To still others he was a great guerrilla fighter who fought for the good of the poor people.

In her efforts to have her husband's name honored, Luz de Villa was helped by some of Pancho Villa's former followers who were still alive. They were called *Dorados*, "Golden, or Shining, Ones." She finally won her fight, and in 1967, after a long debate, the Mexican Congress declared Villa a hero of the Revolution of 1910.

Pancho Villa was born on June 5, 1878 in Rio Grande, Durango, one of the northern Mexican states. His real name was

Doroteo Arango. He was the son of a poor farm worker. Like many other children of the poor in country districts of those days, young Doroteo lived by his wits. Attendance at school was not compulsory. He wandered about, begged, and even became a petty thief. When he was about twelve, his father died. When he was seventeen, he killed a farm owner, because of some wrong done to him or to his sister. For this he was declared an outlaw and arrested. He escaped and joined a bandit named Ignacio Parra. At this time Doroteo Arango changed his name to Francisco, or Pancho, Villa after the name of an earlier bandit of that region. *Pancho* is the pet name for *Francisco.*

Other bandits were roaming over the countryside, or hiding in the mountains, desert regions, and forests. Their leaders found recruits among the poor, who saw no hope of a better life, and among those who were in trouble with the law and felt that they could not get a fair trial.

The country was suffering under the long tyranny of Porfirio Díaz. The rich were becoming richer, while the poor were losing all hope that land reforms would be carried out. Foreign companies were given rights in Mexico, and they paid their workers very little.

Under these conditions bandit leaders like Villa were able to attract many men to their side. He left Parra and joined other leaders, especially Tomás Urbina, who later became one of his generals. Villa then built up a large army under his own command.

When he was 32, an event took place that changed his entire life, and led to his becoming a world-wide figure—the Revolution of 1910. Díaz was forced to resign; Francisco Madero became President in 1911.

Villa felt that Madero was the answer to Mexico's problems, that he would carry out a program to help the poor. Villa's own way of life had changed. He was now a successful commander who had helped bring about the change in government. Now having some money, he was a more settled person, but he still was on the side of the poor.

He was not happy with the men who aided Madero in the government. He decided to retire on a ranch he now owned. Later, he went into the meat business, opening a store in the city of Chihuahua.

In 1911 he married. The story of how he met his bride is told in her own words in the *New York Times* of April 27, 1969.

"My parents had a general store in the little town of San

Porfirio Díaz

Andrés. On November 21, 1910, Pancho rode into the town at the head of his troops, several hundred of them on horseback, and one of his captains came into the store, covered with dust.

"He asked my mother for a loan of the money in the till. We were very frightened, because we had only a little money and said we needed that to pay our debts . . .

" 'I will report that to the men outside,' said the captain.

"I went with him. My mother thought we would be robbed of all we had . . . The captain took me to Pancho, and I told him how little money we had, and how we needed it. He said, 'Okay, then just give me your food stock to feed my boys. They're worn out.'

"That was how we met. Six months later, in May 1911, we were

Monument of the Revolution, Mexico City

married in our village church."

Villa did not remain in retirement very long. Madero wrote to him several times, and called upon him for advice. Villa visited Madero in Mexico City twice, and then came out of retirement to help him.

The President had placed the cruel and treacherous General Victoriano Huerta in command of the army. He plotted with the enemies of Madero to overthrow him, accused Villa of disobeying him, had him arrested, and sentenced him to be shot, without giving him a chance to defend himself. On the night before the execution, a friend of Villa, Raoul Madero, brother of the President, managed to get a message by telegram to the President.

On the morning of June 3, 1912, Villa was taken before a firing squad. At first he thought the whole affair was a joke, that Huerta was trying to frighten him. Soon he realized that Huerta was serious. A scene followed like something from a movie. Six men armed with rifles stood ready to fire, when suddenly, two men on horseback galloped up and shouted, "Wait! Don't fire! " One rider was Raoul Madero, with an answer to his telegram. The President had ordered the execution stopped!

However, Villa was not set free. He was taken to Mexico City as a prisoner. This experience made him very bitter and distrustful. He decided always to be armed, and absolutely careful about any agreements made with leaders of the Government.

He was placed in the Federal Penitentiary in Mexico City as a prisoner of war, charged with refusing to obey his superiors and taking money. His defense was that the money had been taken from bankers to pay the soldiers, because the Government had not been paying them.

Villa remained in prison six months. He had never gone to school, but in prison he learned to read and write and studied the history of Mexico. On December 26, 1912, he made a sensational escape. With help from the outside, he disguised himself, walked out, went all the way to the border, and reached El Paso, Texas.

In Mexico, there were uprisings against Madero. The President and his brother were killed early in 1913. Huerta became President. Opposition to him was great. Villa returned to Mexico to take up the fight against him, becoming the head of an army called the Division of the North.

Villa won great victories in 1913 and 1914. He captured the cities of Chihuahua, Juárez, Monterrey, Saltillo, and Torreón. He worked together with Alvaro Obregón, a very able military leader, who led the revolt against Huerta in the state of Sonora in the north. Villa attracted to his side men of all kinds, from former bandits to aristocrats.

However, the leader of the revolt turned out to be a landowner, Venustiano Carranza. He and Villa were the only leaders fighting against Huerta who wanted to become President, but neither could gain the necessary support.

Meanwhile, the United States took an interest in what was going on in Mexico. Americans felt great sympathy for the Constitutionalists, as Huerta's opponents were called, and volunteers rushed to help them. At first President Woodrow Wilson did not allow weapons or ammunition to be shipped to Mexico, because he wanted to weaken Huerta's cause. After an insult to American sailors at Veracruz, the city was seized by an American fleet, and almost 200 Mexicans defending it were killed. However, to help the Constitutionalists, President Wilson re-opened the shipment of weapons.

CONSTITUCION
1917 POLITICA 1967

CARRANZA
AEREO
MEXICO 80¢

Venustiano Carranza

Villa and Obregón now rushed toward Mexico City with their armies. Huerta fled the country. Obregón entered Mexico City in triumph, getting there ahead of Villa. On November 27, 1914, Villa and Emiliano Zapata, the two greatest popular leaders of the Revolution of 1910, met for the first time at Xochimilco, close to Mexico City. On December 6, riding on their horses, they led a combined army of about 50,000 men in a victory parade through Mexico City.

This must have been the proudest moment of Villa's life. He had come a long way from being a peon, a bandit, and an outlaw. Now he was one of the leaders of his country with the power to decide who would be President. He might be President himself! He must have felt that he belonged in the President's chair, for when photographers taking pictures in the National Palace asked him to sit in it and pose, he did so.

Delegates to a convention called together to choose a new President could not decide between Villa and Carranza. Villa suggested that the country could have peace if both he and Carranza would commit suicide, but Carranza turned down this way of settling the problem. For the time being, Eulalio Gutiérrez was named Acting President. He appointed Villa his military commander, and Carranza left Mexico City.

The armies of Villa and Zapata were really in control of the city. Villa's men ran wild, plundering and killing, and even Villa could not stop them. Acting President Gutiérrez, also unable to do anything, fled Mexico City.

Villa was winning support in the United States. He did not drink or smoke, and for that reason he was favored by Secretary of State Williams Jennings Bryan and others like him who also were neither drinkers nor smokers! Even some American business-men favored Villa because they thought that he would be easier to control than Carranza. On the other hand, Villa, lost the support of General Obregón, who thought that Carranza had a real program but that Villa had none.

Life in Mexico City did not please Vilia, who was used to open fields and mountains. As General Obregón, who had taken up arms in support of Carranza, was approaching Mexico City, Villa went back north. General Ángeles and his artillery-men fought for Villa; it was said that as long as he was on Villa's side, Villa never lost a battle. However, Ángeles left for New York and did not return to Mexico until 1918.

Villa now lost battle after battle. American support was withdrawn when Wilson and Bryan decided to back Carranza. Villa was defeated by Obregón in a long and bloody battle at Celaya on April 6, 1915. Towns held by his men were given up, and many of his followers deserted. Villa became a bandit chief again and fled to his native state of Chihuahua where the people looked upon him almost as an idol.

He blamed the United States for his failure to become President and for his defeats, accusing President Wilson of "double-crossing" him by supporting Carranza. In revenge he began raids across the border, and held up trains in Mexico, killing American passengers. Americans along the border fought back unofficially and killed in return.

Villa's most famous raid was made in March 1916, when he crossed into New Mexico and killed more than fifteen inhabitants of the town of Columbus, burned buildings, and robbed stores. President Wilson ordered General John J. Pershing and a force to Mexico to catch Villa "alive or dead."

However, Villa was not to be caught so easily. He knew the country much better than did the Americans following him, and there were people there who warned him and helped him to escape. Also, some Mexicans were angry at what they considered American interference in their affairs. Even Carranza, who was now President of Mexico, refused to help capture Villa, although he was his enemy. He wanted the Americans out of the country. Villa became a hero to many Mexicans. His attacks on American citizens, even the murder of innocent persons, were looked upon as acts of revenge for what the Americans had done in Veracruz. General Pershing finally had to return to the United States.

Villa carried on his fight against Carranza from 1916 to 1920, as long as Carranza was President. But the fight was no longer a revolution; it had no real meaning. Most of Villa's old allies and leaders were dead. General Zapata and General Ángeles had been murdered. Villa took towns but was not strong enough to hold them. He lived as a raider and a bandit.

Finally, Carranza himself was the victim of treachery at the hands of General Obregón. Adolfo de la Huerta, (not related to the former President) was chosen as temporary President. He offered Villa a pardon. First, Villa took the town of Sabinas to have a strong position, and then he bargained with de la Huerta. He was tired of the long fight and felt that he could trust the new President. He was not called upon to surrender, but to go into retirement. He accepted. The date was July 28, 1920; he was then 42.

Villa was given a large hacienda in Canutillo, in the State of Durango, where he lived with his wife and children. A bodyguard of fifty men, loyal Dorados, was granted to him. He became a farmer and cattle raiser. He acquired the latest farm machinery: tractors, threshing machines, and plows, also two automobiles. He owned property, including a house and a hotel in the town of Parral.

He led a quiet life as a businessman and landowner, trying to improve conditions for the people of the neighborhood and those working for him. However, there were still men in Mexico who feared Villa. They believed that some day he might come out of retirement to fight against the Government and General Plutarco Elías Calles, who was to run for President in 1924. One of these men, a young rancher named Melitón Losoya, got together seven others to assassinate Villa.

One day, Villa went to Parral on business. He drove his car himself. Five men went along as his bodyguard. Losoya and his men knew that Villa used to go to Parral, and they waited in ambush in a building on a street by which Villa usually drove out. One man was stationed on the street as a lookout. The others waited in the house until the lookout raised his hat as a signal that Villa's car was coming. As the car drew near, rifle shots rang out.

Villa was hit. As he tried to control the car, the men rushed out of the building and shot down his companions. Villa killed one of the assassins, but he himself was hit at least a dozen times. He died on the spot. The date was July 23, 1923; Villa was 47 years old. Villa was buried in Parral. His murderers were never tried

The motion picture *Viva Villa* gives a portrait of Pancho Villa that is different from that of the real man. He was a tall man with a mustache, reddish hair, and deep, bright brown eyes. He had dash and liveliness. Usually he wore khaki outfits, a large sombrero, or straw hat, and almost always carried a gun. In his favorite photograph of himself he is wearing a plain suit, but his hat is not the usual high sombrero.

Pancho Villa on his horse, Seven Leagues

Even in his lifetime Pancho Villa had become a legend. Songs called *corridos,* a form of ballad, are very popular in Mexico. They tell about events and people in the news. Many were written about Villa. The writers of *corridos* told the truth about the heroes. They did not glorify them. They told about their good qualities, but they also sang about their weaknesses.

That is how the story of Pancho Villa has to be told and remembered. He has been called a Robin Hood, an Attila the Hun, a savage barbarian, a Jesse James, an outlaw. It is true that he broke the law, stole, and murdered. He also had his tender moments, and could win the loyalty of faithful followers. He could be soft, and he could be cruel. He had ideals and a dream of helping the poor. The strange part of his life is that when he had given up fighting and was leading a peaceful life, he was killed by men against whom he had not fought, but who feared him for what he had been and for what he might still be!

Alvaro Obregón and Pancho Villa

15

EMILIANO ZAPATA

FIGHTER FOR LAND AND FREEDOM

On April 10, 1969, Mexico honored the memory of one of her greatest revolutionaries, Emiliano Zapata. That day was the fiftieth anniversary of his assassination. President Gustavo Díaz Ordaz placed a wreath on the statue of the man who fought for land and freedom in the Revolution of 1910.

Zapata was born on August 8, 1877 (or 1879) in the village of Anenecuilco in the state of Morelos, south of Mexico City. Zapata was a mestizo. He had three sisters and an older brother, Eufemio. Their father owned a small piece of land, Emiliano went to a primary school and also helped his father work the land. When the boy was eighteen, his father died. Since Eufemio was now married and living away from the family, Emiliano took care of the little farm and supported his mother and three sisters. He rented a small piece of land from the owner of an hacienda and raised watermelons. He was also able to buy some mules which he used for hauling corn.

Zapata became an excellent charro, or horseman. Although he lived less than a century ago, legends have sprung up about him. There is a story that the owner of the hacienda, recognizing his ability as a horseman and his interest in horses, sent him to Mexico City to look at his paddock, the place where his horses were kept. Zapata looked at the beautiful stables, and saw what good care was given to the horses. The floors and walls were covered with expensive tiles, and the places in which the horses were washed were lined with marble.

Zapata thought of the difference between the treatment of the horses and that of the Indians working on the haciendas in his state. He compared the tiles and marbles in the horses' stables with the poor huts in which the Indians lived and the rags they wore. The injustice of their treatment and poverty angered him.

Such is the story, but Zapata did not really need this trip to Mexico City to become aware of the problems of the poor. At home, under the rule of Porfirio Díaz, owners of haciendas were taking away the *ejidos* and making them part of their own property. An *ejido* was a piece of land owned in common by the people of a village. The right of the Indians to hold *ejidos* had existed for centuries, even before the Spaniards conquered Mexico.

Another part of the Zapata story is that he and his brother also lost the small pieces of land that they owned. Zapata and others in the village had long been crying out against the system whereby the poor were losing their land, and he was considered to be dangerous by Díaz's authorities in the district. Several times he was forced to leave the village.

In 1909, Zapata was elected by the villagers to head a committee to defend their rights. The local representatives of President Díaz, the Governor of Morelos, and President Díaz himself refused to do anything for them. Zapata gathered about him a number of faithful followers who were ready to fight to win back the land that had been taken from them.

When the Revolution of 1910 broke out, Zapata's men attacked the political chiefs of Díaz in the towns and villages, and seized land, shooting those who tried to stop them. They were burning with the spirit of revenge and a desire to make up for the injustices committed against them. The troops sent against them robbed and murdered, trying to put down the revolt by terror.

Zapata became an important leader in the Revolution of 1910. His army was known as the Division of the South, but his followers, the *Zapatistas,* called it the Liberator Army of the South. Zapata was a great guerrilla leader who was worshiped by

Zapata, holding sombrero; Villa, in president's chair

his men and by the peasants of the districts he occupied. He understood their problems and showed great consideration for the people. One of the reasons he was so hard to defeat on his home grounds was that the people there organized to help him.

At the beginning of the Revolution, Zapata gained a number of victories and captured the cities of Cuernavaca and Cuautla. Zapata differed from Villa and other leaders. He did not want power for himself; he would accept no gifts of land or other favors. Unlike Villa, Zapata refused to pose for a picture in the President's chair. He had one great idea for which he fought all his life: to get back for the poor, especially the Indians, the land that had been taken away from them over the centuries, and to bring back their old way of life. His slogan was: *Tierra y Libertad,* "Land and Liberty."

Zapata did not trust politicians to carry out their promises, although he did agree to wait when Madero became President. When he saw that nothing was being done, he formed his own plan, the famous Plan of Ayala, which was drawn up on November 28, 1911. It received its name from Ayala, a small place near Cuautla.

In this Plan, Zapata wanted the land taken away from the Indians by the landlords to be given back to them. The Plan of Ayala also called for granting one-third of the land of the hacienda to the peasants. The landowners and also Carranza opposed this plan. Zapata must have realized that he could not get his program through without force, since one of his declarations was: "Seek justice from tyrannical governments, not with your hat in your hands but with a rifle in your fist."

Zapata gave the ideas for the full Plan, which was then put into written form by a schoolmaster, Otilio Montaño. Many men of education and learning were attracted to Zapata's ideas. Dr. José G. Parres, who later became Governor of Morelos and served in high offices of the Government, offered his services as a doctor. The leading intellectual who helped Zapata was Antonio Díaz Soto y Gama, the greatest orator of his time. He praised Zapata very highly and spoke in his favor at conventions. Zapata's proclamations were written in clear and beautiful language; many of them were the work of Gama and other intellectual supporters.

However, Zapata, who had never had any higher education, had a bright, clear mind and could express himself in stirring language. His memorable sayings show his spirit and what he was fighting for.

"The Land and Liberty, the land free for all, land without overseers and without masters, is the war cry of the Revolution."

The next quotation shows how clearly he understood what happens to the reputation of men like himself who have fought against the power of the established order to bring about change.

"The enemies of the country and of freedom of the people have always given the name bandits to those who sacrifice themselves for the noble causes of the people."

His independence is shown by this declaration: "I want to die a slave to principles, not to men."

Finally, there is the sentence which his men are said to have written on the walls of Mexico City:

"Men of the South, it is better to die on your feet than to live on your knees! "

Zapata took part in the Victory Parade with Villa in Mexico City on December 6, 1914. The inhabitants of Mexico City expected the worst from Zapata's men. They had heard about him as a bandit; they thought that his Indians were lawless savages. Instead, they turned out to be gentle and law-abiding—so unlike Villa's men. They went about the city looking at everything like sightseers. The story goes that they knocked at the doors of the rich and quietly asked for water and food.

After the defeat of Villa at Celaya, Zapata and his men blocked the roads near Mexico City and made attacks on it, but they finally had to retreat to the south. There they carried on the fight against Carranza for three years. As before, they were unbeatable on their own ground.

Finally, the federal government used treachery to overcome Zapata, just as an earlier government has used it against Guerrero. General Pablo González, with a few thousand soldiers, came against Zapata, who had only a few hundred men. González was known as "the general who had never won a victory." Moreover, he was very cruel. He and his men did more damage to the farms than the Zapatistas had ever done. Zapata's men plowed the fields they took; González's soldiers destroyed, burned, and robbed; González himself became rich by selling his share of the plunder.

Jesús Guajardo, a colonel in González's army, spread rumors that he wanted to desert to Zapata with 800 men. This came to Zapata's attention. Meetings were arranged between him and the Colonel. Zapata did not trust Guajardo and asked for proof of his desire to desert, suggesting that the Colonel capture a place held by the troops of González. Guajardo attacked this place, took it, and then, to show Zapata that he was sincere, ordered the prisoners shot! He and his superiors were willing to kill their own men in cold blood to capture one man like Zapata!

Zapata now believed Guajardo, who arranged to have him come to dine with him at an hacienda near Cuautla. On April 10, 1919, Zapata went there with a small group of men. Guajardo had stationed an honor guard at the entrance to receive the visitors. Bugles were blown, and the soldiers of the guard raised their rifles as a salute. At the command "Present arms! " the soldiers of the guard fired, killing Zapata and all his men! Colonel Guajardo was promoted to Brigadier General and was given a large sum of money. President Carranza said he knew nothing about the plot, but Guajardo was never punished for killing his own soldiers.

Mural of Zapata in classroom, Cuernavaca

In the state of Morelos, there is a legend that Zapata never really believed Guajardo, that he went off to China, and still returns to Cuautla every year, unknown to all. He is supposed to take part in the celebration there every April 10th, and then disappear. Another legend is that he is still riding his black horse over the mountains, ready to help the peasants of the south whenever they need him.

Zapata's fame has grown steadily over the years. He is honored as the leader of the Agrarian Cause, the fight for land and reforms. His ideas are brought up by speakers, and he is looked up to as the one leader of the Revolution of 1910 who fought honestly and steadfastly for an idea, for the rights of the Indians and the other poor of Mexico.

That statue in Cuautla, in which Zapata is seated on a horse, was put up in 1931; it is but one of many of him in Mexico. Diego Rivera painted his picture in the murals in the Ministry of Education Building in Mexico City, and Orozco made a number of paintings of Zapata. Pictures of Zapata appear on many Mexican stamps.

During the Revolution of 1910 more *corridos,* or ballads, were written and sung about Zapata than any other hero of the time. Every May 10 there is a charro festival in Cuautla in honor of Zapata. Hollywood did a film about Zapata in 1952 called *Viva Zapata!* Marlon Brando plays the part of Zapata, and two Mexican-born stars, Anthony Quinn and Margo, appear in it.

Like so many heroes of Mexico, Zapata met his death by bullets. Like so many heroes of Mexico, he did not see his dream come true. He fought a good fight; his ideas and his dream live on and are being worked out peacefully. They could not be killed by bullets!

Emiliano Zapata

114

16

LÁZARO CÁRDENAS

MAN OF THE PEOPLE

Lázaro Cárdenas, President of Mexico from 1934 to 1940, was a new kind of President. Unlike most of those who came before him, he did not become President by force of arms, nor was he driven out of office by a rebellion. Once his term of office was over he left it peacefully, not interfering with the Presidents who came after him.

Lázaro Cárdenas was born on May 21, 1895 in the town of Jiquilpan, in the state of Michoacán. He was one of eight children. His parents, mestizos of Spanish and Tarascan Indian descent, were not rich. His father went into different small businesses and practiced medicine on the side, having learned a little about medicine by himself. His mother took in sewing.

The school in Jiquilpan that young Cárdenas went to had six grades and about 150 pupils, all taught by one very strict teacher. Cárdenas's father was also very strict and did not allow his children to play in the streets.

When Cárdenas, who was a very good student, had finished the six grades, he had to go to work. There was no higher school to which he could go. His father found a job for him as a clerk in a government office. Later his superior opened a printing office; Lázaro went along and became a typesetter. When the boy was about seventeen, his father died of pneumonia. Lázaro, the oldest son, and his mother had to work to support the family.

He was not much more than eighteen when Huerta became President in 1913. Like many other Mexicans, Cárdenas wanted to fight against him. With about twenty-five men from Jiquilpan, he joined one of the armies fighting Huerta, and was soon a captain.

Cárdenas sided with Carranza against Pancho Villa. He was now a lieutenant colonel. General Plutarco Elías Calles, who was fighting for Carranza, praised Cárdenas very highly and called him *El Chamaco,* "The Kid." Cárdenas was only twenty, but he was already an experienced fighter and a high officer!

He remained in military service from 1916 to 1928, during the terms of Presidents Carranza, Obregón, and Calles. In helping to put down a rebellion in February 1924, he was almost fatally wounded and was taken prisoner. He was going to be shot, but the opposing general, Enrique Estrada, was kind to him and set him free.

In 1925, Cárdenas, now a General, was asked by President Calles to become the military commander of Tampico, a port on the Caribbean and the center of the oil industry. This industry was controlled by foreign companies, chiefly American and British. Cárdenas saw how well the foreigners lived, while the Mexican workers were paid very little.

Cárdenas did not want to continue in military service all his life. His aim was to enter politics and carry out reforms. At first he thought of going back to Jiquilpan to run for Mayor. However, in 1927, some friends visited him in Tampico, and said that they wanted him to run for Governor of Michoacán. Learning that the people of his state really wanted him to be their governor, Cárdenas ran for the office and was elected. In September 1928, he took office, at age 33.

Cárdenas had promised to devote himself to the needs of the people. He began to carry out his promises, opening new schools, breaking up large haciendas, and giving the land to the poor. He helped the workers to organize and encouraged the people to come to him with their problems. Often he went among them to listen and talk to them.

Cárdenas became the head of the strongest political party in Mexico, the National Party of the Revolution, or the PNR. In 1932, shortly after his term of office ended, he married Amalia

Solorzano, a beautiful young lady of rich parents. They have two children, a girl named Amalia, and a boy to whom they gave the name of the last Aztec emperor, Cuauhtémoc.

In December 1933, Cárdenas was nominated for the presidency at a convention of the PNR. Although Calles was not President at the time, he was in control and could determine who should be chosen. As the wealthiest man in Mexico, he had slowed down reforms to aid the poor. There was, however, a great demand for Cárdenas, and Calles had to give in. He thought he could control Cárdenas if he should be elected.

The Convention of the Party had drawn up a Six-Year Plan of action. The reason for the six years was that the term of office of the President had been changed from four to six years. In the plan, education was to be broadened to build more schools for the children of Indians, peasants, and workers, without Church control or supervision.

Before the election, Cárdenas traveled all over Mexico speaking to the people about his plans to make changes. This kind of campaign was unusual. The people loved it. He received 2,268,567 votes against only 24,690 for the rival candidate! As President, he began to work for the changes, which were opposed by Calles. Cárdenas did not listen to him, but put his followers out of office. When it seemed that Calles might rebel, Cárdenas acted quickly. He put Calles and twenty of his followers on an airplane and had them flown out of the country!

Some writers have said about President Cárdenas that he was "too good to be true," because he did not drink or smoke, closed the gambling houses, lived simply, cut his salary in half, and turned back to the state the money given to his wife as First Lady. Other heads of Mexico had become rich in office, but Cárdenas acted differently by even giving up part of his land.

He opened night schools for workers in his campaign to teach all how to read and write. He was a great lover of trees, and had them planted everywhere possible. Backward areas were opened up and developed by the building of new roads. Some of these areas were made fertile by irrigation, bringing water to the fields. By dividing large estates, he got more land for the peasants than all the Presidents before him.

On March 18, 1938, Cárdenas took the boldest step of his entire career as President. He expropriated, or took away, the oil industry of all foreign companies and made it the property of the Mexican Government, with a promise to pay for what was taken.

The foreign companies had gotten the oil fields for very little, and gave nothing to the government for the wealth they took out of the ground, besides paying very low wages to the workers. When Cárdenas granted some rights to Shell Oil with the provision the company would pay the workers and the government, the company agreed, but then took its case to the Supreme Court of Mexico. When it lost, it stopped the production of oil, so that Mexican industry suffered. Then Cárdenas went into action.

There was fear that the United States and Great Britain would send troops. However, Great Britain accepted a sum of money in payment. President Franklin D. Roosevelt, who had spoken out for the Good Neighbor Policy, which meant that the United States would have friendly relations with all the other countries of North America and South America, did not send troops. Agreements were made, and Mexico took on a huge debt to repay the foreign companies. The oil industry is now owned and managed by the

President Lázaro Cárdenas

Library, University of Mexico

Mexican Government. Cárdenas also expropriated sugar mills and factories for the people.

Cárdenas came into office without the help of rifles and ruled without the help of an army. He made no political prisoners, and there was complete freedom of the press. His policies had the support of the people, especially of the workers, whom he helped organize into unions. However, he did not let any group take over power. Courageous and fearless, he went among the people without a bodyguard.

He looked out for the welfare of the common man, especially the Indians. Known as "The Traveling President," he went to remote villages where he met the people, and they got to know him. He dressed simply on these trips, appearing in short sleeves and wearing a sombrero. He looked like one of the country people, a *campesino*.

When his term of office was over in 1940, he retired to live a quiet life. When Mexico entered World War II, he was called out of retirement to serve his country as Minister of War between 1943 and 1945, and as Commander-in-Chief of the Army in 1945. In 1955, he was awarded the State Peace Prize by his country. He has long been active as a member of a commission to improve the land.

Cárdenas set an example followed by all the presidents who came after him. Each has served his full term of six years, after gaining the office by a peaceful election. Cárdenas showed Mexico how to work for reforms without civil war, and how to achieve better relations with the countries of the western world. He gained respect for Mexico from other nations of the world.

17

JOSÉ CLEMENTE OROZCO

A GREAT ARTIST

Many writers on art call José Clemente Orozco the greatest Mexican painter. Some call him the greatest artist of the Western Hemisphere, and others say that he is the greatest modern painter of the world.

Orozco himself was very modest. In his autobiography he says about his life "there is nothing of special interest in it, no famous exploits or heroic deeds, no extraordinary or miraculous happenings."

Still, much that was exciting did happen to him. He had to overcome hardships and a physical handicap. When he was seventeen, while he was working on a chemical experiment at home, an explosion blew away his left hand and badly damaged his right one, leaving deep scars. His eyesight and hearing were injured, and his health suffered for the rest of his life.

José Clemente Orozco was born on November 23, 1883 in the town of Ciudad Guzmán, in the state of Jalisco. José had an older sister and a younger brother. When José was born, his father was the owner of a few factories. His mother came from a wealthy family. Both parents were believed to be descendants of the Spanish conquerors of Mexico.

121

When José was not yet three, the family moved to Guadalajara, where they lived until 1890. Then they moved to Mexico City where José entered a primary school. Many years later, one of his classmates recalled that he was a quiet, neat, intelligent pupil who did not show off. The schoolmate also noticed that young José was forever drawing little figures called *muñecos*, dolls or puppets. Even before he was old enough to go to school, little José had wanted to be an artist.

In fact, he had asked his mother to take him to an art school, the San Carlos Academy, and to enroll him as a student. His mother understood her son very well because she herself painted pictures for her own amusement. She saw that the boy had ability, and took him to the Academy. The director said he was too young for even elementary school, but later she tried again. José was not yet seven years old.

The director let him attend classes at night, but not as a regular student. The little boy went to elementary school in the daytime, and every night from six to eight he sat in the art classes. Nobody took any notice of him. José listened to the teacher, did the same work as the older boys, but received no help from the teacher.

At the end of a few weeks, the director of the Academy visited the Orozco home and told the mother that José was doing better work than all the older students. He was more talented than some of the teachers, and was allowed to become a regular student. Many good teachers at the Academy had a great influence upon the pupils. They taught them not only art, but also good qualities, a love of books, of parents, of country, and of honor.

On his way to and from the elementary school, young Orozco passed the printing shop of Vanegas Arroyo, where José Guadalupe Posada, the most famous Mexican engraver of that time, worked at illustrating the books and papers Arroyo published. Orozco could look in, and was fascinated as he watched the engraver. He went into the shop, learned from the engraver's assistants how to use color, and spent most of his allowance buying the printed *corridos* illustrated by Posada.

In 1897, when he was almost fourteen, José's parents sent him to an agricultural school. He was not really interested in farming, but he did love the outdoor life. As he learned to draw maps and diagrams, he thought for a while of becoming an architect. It was time to think of earning a living, for the family was no longer well-to-do. Then, before José could finish his studies, his father died. Young Orozco earned his first salary by making drawings for architects and printers.

Back at home in 1900, he entered the National Preparatory School, where he studied until 1904. Winning special prizes in mathematics, he again thought of becoming an architect. However, he finally realized that painting was his true life's work, so he returned to San Carlos Academy.

There he came under the influence of Dr. Atl, whose real name was Gerardo Murillo. He had taken the name *Dr. Atl* without any first name; *Atl* is from an Aztec word for "water." Dr. Atl had a studio in the Academy, visited the classes, and talked to the students about the great paintings he had seen in Europe, especially frescoes, a kind of mural, or painting made on walls. Frescoes are put on wet plaster that has been smeared on the wall. The painter begins his work before it can dry, mixing the paint with water.

Learning in the schools of art usually consisted of copying the works of the European masters. Under Dr. Atl and his followers, this was changed to allow young artists to paint in their own style. To show their pride in their country, they drew Mexican landscapes. They learned more about the tools with which they worked, the canvas on which they painted, and the colors that they used.

These new ideas and ways of painting were like a revolution, a new movement in Mexican art. Many young painters took to the new ideas. Orozco, Diego Rivera, and David Alfaro Siqueiros are the three most famous. The new movement led to a period in Mexican art known as the Mexican Renaissance, a rebirth of great achievements in art.

The year 1910 was the 100th anniversary of the Cry of Dolores. As part of the celebration the Mexican Government decided to hold an exhibition in Mexico City of paintings of the times. The young artists wanted to know why, since this was the anniversary of Mexican Independence, there were no pictures by Mexicans. They were allowed to show their works, and met with great success. With Dr. Atl as their leader, they formed a society called the Artistic Center. They received permission to paint murals at the National Preparatory School in Mexico City. Murals were their choice because these are large, easily seen, and can be understood by almost everyone.

The revolution against President Díaz broke out before work could begin, but Orozco took no part in it. It must be remembered that he had only one hand. What he saw of the war—the suffering it brought, the looting, and the murders—was hateful to him. He grieved for the parents who lost their sons; he was angry at the politicians who "sold out," at so-called liberators who worked for their own interests. These feelings, as well as his sympathy for the underdog, love for Mexico, and desire to improve the conditions of the workers and the poor, are expressed in his paintings. However, he did not take a large and active part in political life, as Orozco and Siqueiros did.

To earn a living he opened a small studio where he did enlargements of portraits. He left for a short time during the occupation of Mexico City by Villa. Dr. Atl, who backed Carranza, won some workers and artists over to his side. They went to Orizaba, where Dr. Atl edited a newspaper in favor of Carranza. Orozco drew caricatures, pictures that exaggerate people's faults in a humorous way.

After Carranza became President, Orozco returned to Mexico City, where he drew caricatures for newspapers. They were so clever that people looked at them before anything else in the paper. In 1917, Orozco decided that conditions were not favorable for an artist and left for the United States. First, he went to San Francisco, where he met many Mexicans and went into business with one of them as a commercial artist. After two years, he traveled to New York where the sights of the big city, especially Harlem and Coney Island, thrilled him.

Back in Mexico, government officials had been helping artists. One improvement was the new National Department of Education, set up in 1921, and headed by José Vasconcelos. New schools, libraries, and other public buildings were being erected. Vasconcelos wanted artists to decorate these buildings with murals, and allowed them to paint as they pleased. Never before had artists had such opportunities in Mexico; theater, restaurant, and hotel owners were also anxious to have murals in their buildings!

There was some public opposition to the subjects of the murals. Students at the Preparatory School objected to them. A group of women who did not like the figure of a naked female in one of Orozco's murals drove him away from his work and covered the paintings.

When Vasconcelos left his position in 1924, the artists found it difficult to continue much longer. One day, students chased Siqueiros and Orozco out of the building where they were painting, and ruined the pictures with knives, clubs, and stones.

Orozco felt that he could not do his best work in Mexico, and in 1927, he decided to leave the country.

José Clemente Orozco

By the sale of a painting and with financial help from Genaro Estrada, Secretary of Foreign Relations, Orozco had enough to get him to New York and to stay there for a few months. At first he lived in a brownstone house on Riverside Drive near Columbia University. He loved to wander about and visit the places he remembered from his first trip, like Harlem. He also discovered the original Ghetto, the lower East Side, where Jews lived, and even went to a Jewish theater. Chinatown and the Italian district on and near Mulberry Street were also neighborhoods he enjoyed.

After he had been in New York about six months, an American writer he had met in Mexico introduced him to Alma Reed, another writer. Orozco was then 45 years old. Alma Reed describes how he looked at the time: younger than his age, slender, and of medium build. He had a small mustache and wavy black hair. His eyes were brown; they seemed to be looking deeply into a person. At times he seemed determined; his jaw was strong and square. Miss Reed was impressed by his sense of humor, and noticed, just as his schoolmate had, that he was very neat, gentle, and mild.

Miss Reed introduced Orozco to Madame Eva Sikelianos, wife of a Greek poet, at whose home he met many of her friends. Madame Sikelianos sat for her portrait, as did some of her friends for theirs. Orozco also sold some of the pictures he had brought with him from Mexico as well as his paintings of New York scenes. He was able to stay longer in New York.

In 1929, Orozco paid a brief visit to his family in Mexico whom he had been unable to take with him to New York. He had married in 1923 and had three children. In 1930, through two Mexican friends in the West, he was asked to paint murals at Pomona College, near Los Angeles. In the meantime, his pictures were being shown at exhibitions in different parts of the country.

On his return to New York he painted frescoes in the New School for Social Research, which was then being put up. One of the subjects is "The Table of Brotherhood," in which the different peoples of the world are seated together in friendship. Orozco painted the murals without receiving any payment because he believed in the aims of the school. Dr. Alvin S. Johnson, head of the New School, called Orozco "the greatest mural painter of our time."

Stephen C. Clark, a noted art collector, saw the murals and declared that Orozco was the greatest modern Mexican painter. He ordered a number of paintings from him, and with the money he received, Orozco sent for his family.

In 1932, Orozco was asked to do a mural for Dartmouth College in New Hampshire, where he worked for two years on panels in the college library. In the summer of 1934, he took a trip

"The Table of Brotherhood"

to Europe, visiting England, France, Spain, and Italy. He was anxious to see the works of the great Spanish and Italian artists of the past.

He was now ready to settle down in Mexico. His family had already returned home. Some of Orozco's greatest work was done in his final years in Mexico. He was called upon to do murals in many cities, for by this time his fame was world-wide.

At his own expense he painted murals in a national shrine in Mexico City, the former chapel of a church that Cortés had built and where he is buried. He also painted murals in the Gabino Ortiz Library in Jiquilpan, birthplace of President Cárdenas, and in the Assembly Hall of the University and the Governor's Palace in Guadalajara—to mention only a few places.

The murals that he painted in the old chapel of the Hospicio Cabañas, an asylum for orphans and old people in Guadalajara, are considered his greatest work. These murals show man, his hopes and fear, and his struggle against nature, as he is battling to overcome forces, and the same forces overcoming him—the good and evil in mankind. One part has a procession of Mexican history and all the types of people that have shaped Mexico.

A few other themes, or subjects, of Orozco's paintings are the horrors of war, man's struggle against poverty, ignorance, and injustice, the fight of the people for food, the misuse of great wealth, the modern meanings of the Bible and myths, the destruction that the Machine Age can bring, and the working together of artists, scientists, workers, and all races and peoples for a better world!

One of his great messages to the Mexican people is seen on the walls of the main entrance of the National College for Teachers in Mexico City. These murals show his hopes for the future of Mexico. Orozco teaches that man must work with his hands and his brain to achieve progress. Children are the true hope of the future, and the school is the place for solving human and national problems. Much remains to be done, and the people must still fight for progress and a better life.

Orozco had a dream of going back to live in his native state. He had a three-story house built as his home and studio in Guadalajara, and had no thought of retiring, but on September 7, 1949, he died suddenly of a heart attack.

The nation mourned his death. The Congress of Mexico declared two days of mourning, and ordered that he should be buried in the *Rotunda de los Hombres Illustres,* "Rotunda of Illustrious Men," a part of a cemetery in Mexico City where many of Mexico's most famous men are buried. This was the first time such an honor was paid to an artist! In 1951, his widow agreed to have his home turned into a museum, which is called *Museo-Taller Orozco,* "Orozco Museum Studio, or Workshop." Every year, on the anniversary of his death, a service in his honor is held there.

Many who knew and wrote about Orozco felt that he was an artist who worked not for himself alone or to please the taste of the moment. His spirit and his ideas were for the nation and all mankind, and for all time!

18

DIEGO RIVERA

REVOLUTIONARY WITH A PAINTBRUSH

The artist Diego Rivera was a giant of the Mexican Renaissance. His name is better-known to many Americans than Orozco's because Rivera's life was more spectacular, and he was involved in many incidents both in the United States and in Mexico that brought him great publicity.

Diego Rivera was born in Guanajuato on December 8, 1886, the older of twin boys. In his autobiography, he writes that through his mother he belonged to three racial groups: white, red, and black. His father's ancestors were Portuguese, Spanish, Italian, Russian, and Jewish. One of his ancestors was Uriel Acosta, the famous Portuguese-Jewish philosopher.

Diego's twin brother, Carlos, died when the boys were about a year and a half old. Diego was a thin little boy who suffered from rickets. His health was very bad, and the doctor advised his father to send him to the country. When Diego was two, he was sent to live with an Indian nurse named Antonia. The boy's mother was too upset by the death of Carlos to do anything for Diego.

Antonia lived in a small hut in the woods on a mountain, and let the boy roam about as he wished. He made friends of the animals in the forest, and near the house he kept a pet goat that gave him milk. When he was four years old, Diego returned home strong and healthy.

When he was six years old, one of his ambitions was to become an engineer. Everyone called him "The Engineer" because he was so fond of mechanical toys. He also loved to watch the trains and began to draw them as well as machines.

The family moved to Mexico City, Diego was seven. His father had lost his money, and they had to live in a poor neighborhood. Diego entered school at the age of eight, and thought at that time that he would like to go to a military school. He was good at drawings maps and making plans of battle. However, what he really wanted was to become an artist.

At the age of eleven, he studied at an elementary school in the daytime and went to the San Carlos Academy at night. After two years, he won a scholarship, and from then on went only to art school by day. He got high marks, and won every prize offered, but he was not happy with the work. What he wanted was a new kind of study, like the art of the Mexican Indians before their conquest by the Spaniards.

Other students felt the same, and Rivera organized a strike. He writes that it was really a protest against President Porfirio Díaz. The strike turned into a riot, and Rivera was expelled because he was the leader. That was the end of his training in any school. Never again did he have anything to do with an academy, except for a few months as director of San Carlos years later.

Diego was now sixteen years old. He was short and fat, but he had tremendous energy. His father obtained a grant of money for him from Teodoro A. Dehesa, Governor of Veracruz, a liberal person, interested in art. Diego studied by himself. Like Orozco, he learned much from the engraver José Guadalupe Posada.

Rivera also met Dr. Atl, who had just returned from Europe and filled Rivera with a desire to go there. In 1905, when he was nineteen, Rivera told Governor Dehesa about his wish. The Governor advised him to have a showing of his paintings so that he might sell them. Then he would help the young artist with money for the trip and living expenses in Europe. Rivera painted for an entire year; Dr. Atl prepared the show for him. It was a great success with every painting sold! Governor Dehesa then gave Rivera the money as he had promised.

Before he left for Europe, something happened that affected his ideas and his work for the rest of his life. He was painting near Mt. Orizaba where there were textile mills nearby. The workers received very low wages, and the owners and managers could beat them. In the winter of 1906, the owners passed new rules that made the life of the workers even more miserable, and they went on strike.

Diego Rivera

President Díaz was asked to help them, and promised to do something. He did, but not for them. He sent soldiers who shot the Indians down. The walkout went on, and Rivera put down his paintbrushes and joined the strikers. The soldiers used their sabers against the crowd. A mounted policeman hit Rivera across his skull. He never forgot what happened on that day and often painted such scenes.

Rivera was put into prison with the strikers, but was soon released. The experience made him decide to work for the poor, the discontented, and the oppressed. He called himself "a revolutionary with a paintbrush." At this time, he was twenty years old, more than six feet tall, and weighed 300 pounds!

Rivera remained in Europe almost four years. Traveling through Spain, France, Belgium, and England, he visited art galleries, met other artists, and painted. He earned money by selling some of his paintings abroad; others he sent to Mexico to be sold there.

On his return, Governor Dehesa asked him to have another one-man show. This opened on November 20, 1910, and his great success was repeated. The revolt against President Díaz took place in this year, and Rivera joined Zapata's forces for about six months. Then he left for Europe again, remaining there all through World War I (1914-1918) and until his return to Mexico in 1921.

There he thought changing conditions would be better for his work. New ideas about painting came to him, and he used rich, bright colors, deeper than those he had seen in the European paintings. He saw beauty in the Mexican people, the crowds in the markets, the festivals, and the workers in the fields and factories. Messages of protest against oppression, the rich, and the evils of society were put into his pictures.

The history of Mexico was depicted in his paintings, from the days of the Aztecs down to his own times. The great heroes of the War of Independence and the Revolution of 1910 were on his canvases. He tried to bring back the art of the Aztecs and even used some of the materials they had used.

After his return from Europe, Rivera was asked to do a mural at the National Preparatory School of the University of Mexico. He called it "The Creation." Into it he put all the racial groups that make up the Mexican people, from the ancient Indians to the mestizos. It was completed in the spring of 1922.

At that time he became active politically, joining the Communist Party of Mexico. Rivera wrote for the Party's paper for many years, and helped to form the Syndicate (similar to a union) of Technical Workers, Painters, and Sculptors. Many well-known artists joined. After José Vasconcelos became Minister of Education, Rivera's murals began to appear in many places in Mexico. One of his greatest works appears in the Ministry of Education Building in Mexico City. Others are in the Palace of Cortés in Cuernavaca, with pictures of the Spanish Conquest, Morelos, and Zapata, and in the National Palace in Mexico City.

Rivera made many trips out of Mexico, visiting Germany and the Soviet Union. He painted murals in San Francisco and Detroit, where he met Henry Ford whom he admired for his skill. Rivera had never lost his interest in mechanical things. One of his stories is how he spent a whole day by himself in the Dearborn Museum of Machinery near Detroit looking at the trains and machines. It

"Mother Earth," painting by Rivera

was his idea that man and the machine were greater than the heroes of legend and myth, if only man used the machine to free himself from tiresome, meaningless work. In Detroit he painted murals of the steel, automobile, and chemical industries.

When Rockefeller Center was being built in New York City, Rivera was asked to do a series of murals for the RCA Building. The subject was "Man at the Crossroads Looking with Hope and High Vision to the Choosing of a New and Better Future." Rivera began work on the murals in the spring of 1933.

He painted a night club scene in which the rich were enjoying themselves, while unemployed workers were being hit by police. On the opposite side he painted a May Day celebration, workers singing, and girls exercising in a stadium. Over them was Lenin, leader of the Russian Revolution, holding the hands of a black American worker and a Russian soldier and worker. These were to be the allies of the future, the bringers of brotherhood and peace.

Rivera said that Nelson Rockefeller, representing John D. Rockefeller, Jr., had seen the sketches beforehand. However, as the mural was being painted, there were objections to the scenes, especially the picture of Lenin. Rockefeller had the work stopped, paid Rivera in full, and later had the murals destroyed. A few years later, Rivera painted the murals again in the Palace of Fine Arts in Mexico City, changing the title to "Man at the Crossroads, Looking with Uncertainty but with Hope to a Better World," and adding an unflattering picture of John D. Rockefeller, Jr., "to get even."

In 1952, Rivera developed cancer, but a short trip to Europe seemed to help him. In 1954, tragedy hit him. His wife, Frida Kahlo Rivera, also an artist, died after a long illness. Rivera's cancer returned, and he visited Russia, where a new treatment was being tried. The Russian doctors declared him cured, and he began to paint with as much energy as before. However, in November 1957, his heart began to fail. He died on November 25, 1957. Like Orozco, he was honored with burial in the same cemetery where many of Mexico's illustrious men are buried.

Rivera's seventy-one years were filled with activity and excitement. His power, originality, and genius gave his paintings a heroic grandeur that has earned him everlasting fame among the artists of Mexico and the world.

19

CARLOS CHÁVEZ

MEXICO'S FOREMOST COMPOSER

When Americans think of Mexican music, it is usually of folk music, of popular and dance music. They may have an idea of bands dressed in colorful costumes, of mariachi musicians, the street entertainers, or of players on the marimba, an instrument struck with something like a hammer. They may have heard the music of the *Jarabe Tapatío,* the Mexican national dance, known here as the Mexican Hat Dance.

The Mexicans have had a long history of popular and folk music. You have read about the *corridos* in the chapters on Villa and Zapata. During the days of these two leaders, *La Cucaracha* "The Cockroach," the song of Villa's men, was sung, hummed, or whistled here; *Adelita,* the song of Zapata's men, was almost as popular. Among the many other songs of the revolutionaries of 1910, two are especially memorable, *Cielito Lindo*, "Pretty Little Heaven," and *Río Rosa*, "Rose River." Much later, Americans liked *El Rancho Grande*, "The Big Ranch," sung by Tito Guizar in a Mexican cowboy movie. The song *Estrellita* by Manuel M. Ponce is well-known here, as are the waltzes originally written for the piano, *Over the Waves (Sobre las Olas)*, by Juventino Rosas. Agustín Lara, composer of *Granada* and *María Bonita*, is a famous composer of Mexican popular songs. The most renowned song writer of Mexico was a woman, María Grever, who wrote 873 songs, and was awarded the Civil Merit Medal as a prize.

But music is not all of one kind, based on folk lore and popular tunes. There is another kind of music, often called "more serious music," of which symphonic music is an example. Mexico, of course, has composers of such music, and among them, Carlos Chávez is the foremost.

Chávez was born near Mexico City on June 13, 1899. His parents were Creoles; he was their seventh child. His father died in 1902, and his mother struggled to support the family. Chávez praised his mother highly in these words, "My mother was able to give us all a beautiful life and education, with limitations, but without misery."

Piano lessons were given to Carlos by his older brother and private teachers, among them the composer Ponce. He studied musical texts and scores by himself without going to music school, began to compose short pieces for the piano at age nine, and at sixteen, he composed two popular piano pieces. At eighteen, he composed a symphony. Chávez himself has said that the number of his early compositions is enormous.

He has also said that his surroundings are a part of every composer. When he looked at the monuments that the Indians had left behind them, he began to think about their music. He also thought about the folk music of his country as a part of himself. The simple melodies of native music, the sudden changes of mood and rhythm, and especially the use of percussion instruments, like the drums in Indian music, appealed to him.

In 1921, José Vasconcelos, Minister of Education, asked him to compose a work. Chávez wrote the music for a ballet, *El Fuego Nuevo*, "The New Fire," based on Aztec subjects. Critics and audiences praised it highly. Chávez then went to Europe for a year, where he became familiar with the work of the modern composers Igor Stravinsky, Arnold Schoenberg, and Francis Poulenc. Chávez called Stravinsky the *maestro* (master) and says he had a great influence on him.

Upon his return to Mexico in 1923, Chávez organized the first concerts of modern music ever given there. Then he went to New

136

York, where he met the American composer Aaron Copland, a man of his own age. The two became great friends, for both had the same aim: to compose music characteristic of their country.

In 1927, Chávez composed a ballet about the conflict of life in North America, and later this music was used for a ballet called *H.P.,* "Horse Power." Diego Rivera designed the costumes and background scenes, and Leopold Stokowski conducted at its first performance, given in the United States in 1932.

In 1928, Chávez was very active in Mexico, not only as a composer but also as a conductor, organizer, teacher, and director. He founded the National Opera of Mexico. As director of the National Conservatory of Music until 1934, he "shook up musical life," as he himself has said. He encouraged musical education in general, but he also had a special class in "musical creation," in which he taught young musicians how to compose. No books were used; the class was like a workshop. He believed that the students could "learn music by learning to make music."

From 1928 to 1952, he was the conductor of the Symphony Orchestra of Mexico, renamed the National Symphony Orchestra. He brought to the Mexican audiences music that they had never heard before. In the words of Aaron Copland, "He taught the people how to listen." Some of the music was new to the players in the orchestra also. Chávez was demanding as a conductor but patient. Above all, he "let the music speak for itself." Soon, tourists who heard him conduct in Mexico City came back with reports of a most thrilling musical evening. Part of the time, from 1933 to 1939, Chávez was kept busy as director of the Institute of Fine Arts.

Like Orozco and Rivera among the painters, Chávez was a giant of the Mexican Renaissance among the musicians. He declared that Mexico had to assert itself in music as well as in the other arts. Like the painters, he and other musicians sometimes went back to Mexican-Indian subjects. Chávez has written many compositions of this kind, including his early work *El Fuego Nuevo.* One of his most famous compositions is *Sinfonía India,* "Indian Symphony," written in 1935, in which he uses Indian melodies and instruments. The name of another work, *Xochipilli Macuilxóchitl,* written in 1945, is a clue to the use of Indian music; it makes great use of percussion instruments.

This kind of music is only a small part of Chávez's enormous number of compositions in many styles and forms. He has described his music as not only Mexican but as North American also, although he has felt the Aztec within himself. He has used the old, or classical style, and the modern style. Some of his music is for the voice as well as for instruments. He organized the first choral concerts in Mexico, and wrote music for choral groups. His works include music for operas, ballets, piano, violin, horns, guitar, and he has composed symphonies, trios, quartets, concertos, and sonatas. He even wrote music for a *corrido*.

All his music is colorful and powerful. Aaron Copland has described it as never being over-romantic or "gooey," but clearly designed, clear-cut without shadows.

A good example of his classical style is the *Sinfonía de Antígona,* "Symphony of Antigone," a title coming from the play *Antigone* by the ancient Greek writer Sophocles. Chávez also wrote music to accompany a modern treatment of this play by the French writer Jean Cocteau. José Limón used the symphonic music for a ballet with costumes and scenery by the great Mexican artist Miguel Covarrubias.

Chávez has written some compositions to be played first before American audiences. Among these are the *Sixth Symphony,* written in 1964, and first conducted by Leonard Bernstein, and a string quartet written in 1965 for the Festival of Arts in Washington, D.C.

Chávez has been a guest conductor in European cities, in many large cities of South America, and in at least thirty cities in Canada and the United States. He also delivered lectures at Harvard in 1959. These lectures were put into a book called *Musical Form,* which gives his ideas on musical composition. In 1937, he had written *Toward a New Music* on the same topic.

Praise comes to Chávez everywhere as a perfectionist, an inspiring leader who gives an "imaginative, emotional, and thrilling performance." He makes an imposing appearance on the conductor's stand, as he is tall, well-built, lively, and energetic. His deep-set brilliant eyes beneath very thick, bushy, dark eyebrows are very impressive, as are his rugged features with a sharp, strong chin, and some gray hair with a few dark patches above his high forehead. He expresses himself well and has a good sense of humor.

Chávez lives in Mexico City. His wife is a former pianist, Otilia Ortiz, whom he married in 1922. They have a son and two daughters.

Now past his seventieth birthday, he is as busy as ever. There

Carlos Chávez

are more demands on his time than he can possibly meet; he is constantly being invited to conduct or to write for special occasions. For example, in 1969, he conducted the Houston Symphony playing his new piece *Elatio* on February 24—another first for an American audience—and later that same year, he wrote *Discovery,* still another new piece for an American audience. This composition was played at the Cabrillo Festival in Aptos, California, on August 24, for the first time in the world.

No other Mexican musician has done for Mexico what Chávez has done. No other Mexican conductor has done as much for music there as he has. He brought the music of the world to Mexico, and Mexican music to the world!

On this note the procession of Mexican heroes comes to an end, or rather, it comes full circle. Our first was a legendary hero who brought culture to his people, the ancient Indians of Mexico. Our last three heroes also brought culture to their people, and although living in modern times, often went back for inspiration and subject matter to the art or music of the ancient Mexican Indians.

INDEX